P9-BYN-665

DK

EYEWITNESS TRAVEL GUIDES

ITALIAN
PHRASE BOOK

A Dorling Kindersley Book

LONDON, NEW YORK, MUNICH,
MELBOURNE, AND DELHI

Compiled by Lexus Ltd with Karen McAulay and Mariarosaria Cardines

Published in the United States by DK Publishing, Inc.
375 Hudson Street
New York, New York 10014

First American Edition 1998
Reprinted with corrections 2000, 2003
2 4 6 8 10 9 7 5 3

Dorling Kindersley books can be purchased in bulk quantities at discounted prices
for use in promotions or as premiums. We are also able to offer special editions
and personalized jackets, corporate imprints, and excerpts from all of our books,
tailored specifically to meet your own needs. To find out more, please contact:
Special Markets Department, Dorling Kindersley Publishing, Inc.,
375 Hudson Street, New York, New York 10014; Fax: 212-689-5254.

Library of Congress Cataloging-in-Publication Data
Italian phrase book. -- 1st American ed.
       p.   cm. -- (Dorling Kindersley travel guide phrase books)
First published in Great Britain in 1997
by Dorling Kindersley Ltd.
Includes index.
ISBN-13: 978-0-7894-9489-4 (alk. paper)
ISBN-10: 0-7894-9489-2 (alk. paper)

   1. Italian language--Conversation and phrase books--
English.   I. DK Publishing, Inc.   II. Series.
PC1121.I855 1998
458.3'421--DC21   97–47227
                                                        CIP

Printed and bound in China by Leo Paper Products Limited

see our complete catalog at
www.dk.com

CONTENTS

PREFACE

This *Dorling Kindersley Eyewitness Travel Guides Phrase Book* has been compiled by experts to meet the general needs of tourists and business travelers. Arranged under headings such as Hotels, Driving, and so forth, the ample selection of useful words and phrases is supported by a 2,000-line mini-dictionary. There is also an extensive menu guide listing approximately 600 dishes or methods of cooking and presentation.

Typical replies to questions you may ask during your trip, and the signs or instructions you may see or hear, are shown in tinted boxes. In the main text, the pronunciation of Italian words and phrases is imitated in English sound syllables. The Introduction provides guidelines to Italian pronunciation.

Dorling Kindersley Eyewitness Travel Guides are recognized as the world's best travel guides. Each title features specially commissioned color photographs, detailed maps, cutaways of major buildings and 3-D aerial views, plus information on sights, events, hotels, restaurants, shopping, and entertainment.

Dorling Kindersley Eyewitness Travel Guides titles include:
Italy · Florence & Tuscany · Milan & the Lakes · Naples · Rome
Sardinia · Sicily · Venice & the Veneto · Amsterdam · Australia
Sydney · Berlin · Budapest · California · Florida · Hawaii
New York · San Francisco & Northern California · Canada · France
Loire Valley · Paris · Provence · Great Britain · London · Ireland
Dublin · Scotland · Greece: Athens & the Mainland · The Greek Islands
Istanbul · Jerusalem & the Holy Land · Mexico · Moscow
St. Petersburg · Portugal · Lisbon · Prague · South Africa
Spain · Barcelona · Madrid · Seville & Andalusia
Thailand · Vienna · Warsaw

INTRODUCTION

PRONUNCIATION

The pronunciation of an Italian word is very similar to the way it is written. When reading the imitated pronunciation, stress the part that is underlined. Pronounce each syllable as if it formed part of an English word and you will be understood. Remember the points below, and your pronunciation will be even closer to the correct Italian.

ai	as in "fair"
ay	as in "pay"
e	as in "bed"
	(pronounced as a separate syllable at the end of a word)
g	always hard as in "get"
I	as in "I"
ow	as in "cow"
r	always strongly pronounced
y	always pronounced as in "yet," except in *ay* as above

Note that when there are two identical consonants separated by a hyphen, eg. **vorrei**—*vor-ray*, both consonants must be pronounced as if you were pronouncing two separate English words: eg. "just two," "full length."

GENDERS AND ARTICLES

Italian has two genders for nouns—masculine and feminine. In the vocabulary section of this book, we generally give the definite article (the). For masculine nouns, the definite article is **il** (plural **i**) before nouns beginning with a consonant, **lo** (plural **gli**) before nouns beginning with "s" + consonant or with "z," and **l'** (plural **gli**) before nouns beginning with a vowel. For feminine nouns, use **la** before a noun beginning with a consonant and **l'** before a vowel (plural **le**).

The masculine indefinite article (a) is **uno** before a noun beginning with a consonant and **un** before a vowel. The feminine is **una** before a consonant and **un'** before a vowel.

USEFUL EVERYDAY PHRASES

YES, NO, OK, ETC.

Yes/No
Sì/No
see/no

Excellent!
Ottimo!
ot-teemo

Don't!
Non farlo!
non farlo

OK
OK
'ok'

That's fine
Va bene
va bene

That's right
È vero
eh vayro

GREETINGS, INTRODUCTIONS

How do you do, pleased to meet you
Piacere di conoscerla
pee-achaire dee konoshairla

Good morning/Good evening/Good night
Buon giorno/Buona sera/Buona notte
bwon jorno/bwona saira/bwona not-te

Goodbye
Arrivederci
ar-reevedairchee

How are you?
Come sta?
kome sta

(familiar)
Come stai?
kome stı

My name is …
Mi chiamo …
mee k-yamo

What's your name?
Come si chiama?
kome see k-yama

(familiar)
Come ti chiami?
kome tee k-yamee

What's his/her name?
Come si chiama?
kome see k-yama

May I introduce …?
Posso presentarle …?
pos-so prezentarle

This is … *(introducing male/female)*
Questo è …/Questa è …
kwesto eh/kwesta eh

Hello
Ciao
chow

Hi!
Salve!
salve

Bye!
Ciao!
chow

See you later
A più tardi
a p-yoo tardee

It's been nice meeting you
Mi ha fatto piacere conoscerla
mee a fat-to pee-achaire konoshairla

PLEASE, THANK YOU, APOLOGIES

Thank you/No, thank you
Grazie/No grazie
gratzee-e/no gratzee-e

Yes, please
Sì, grazie
see gratzee-e

Please *(offering)*　　　　　*(asking for something)*
Prego　　　　　　　　　　　Per favore/per piacere
prego　　　　　　　　　　*pair favore/pair pee-achaire*

Excuse me! *(when sneezing, etc.)*
Scusate!
skoozate

Sorry!　　　　　　　　　　*(familiar)*
Scusi!　　　　　　　　　　　Scusa!
skoozee　　　　　　　　　　*skooza*

I'm really sorry
Sono davvero spiacente
sono dav-vairo spee-achente

It was/wasn't my fault!
È stato/non è stata colpa mia!
eh stato/non eh stata kolpa mee-a

WHERE, HOW, ASKING

Excuse me, please *(to get past, etc.)*
Permesso
pairmesso

Can you tell me ...?
Potrebbe dirmi ...?
potreb-be deermee

Can I have ...?
Potrei avere ...?
potray avaire

Would you like a ...?
Vorrebbe un/una ...?
vor-reb-be oon/oona

Would you like to ...?
Le piacerebbe ...?
le pee-achaireb-be

Is there ... here?
C'è ...?
cheh

What's that?
Che cos'è?
ke kozeh

Where can I get ...?
Dove potrei trovare ...?
dove potray trovare

How much is it?
Quanto costa?
kwanto kosta

Where is the ...?
Dov'è il/la ...?
doveh eel/la

Where is the restroom, please?
Per cortesia, dove sono i gabinetti?
pair kortezee-a dove sono ee gabee-net-tee

Is there wheelchair access?
È possibile l'accesso con la sedia a rotelle?
eh pos-see-bee-leh l'aches-so kon la saidee-a rotail-le

Are there facilities for the disabled?
Ci sono facilità per gli handicappati?
chee sono fachee-lee-ta pair l-yee andee-kap-patee

Are guide dogs allowed?
È permesso portare i cani guida?
eh pairmes-so portarai ee kanee gweeda

ABOUT ONESELF

I'm from …
Sono di …
sono dee

I'm … years old
Ho … anni
o … an-nee

I'm a … *(occupation)*
Faccio il/la …
facho eel/la

I'm married/single/divorced *(said by a man)*
Sono sposato/celibe/divorziato
sono spozato/cheleebe/deevortz-yato

(said by a woman)
Sono sposata/nubile/divorziata
sono spozata/noobeele/deevortz-yata

I have … sisters/brothers/children
Ho … sorelle/fratelli/bambini
o … sorel-le/fratel-lee/bambeenee

Likes, Dislikes, Socializing

I like/love …
Mi piace …
mee pee-<u>a</u>che

I don't like …
Non mi piace …
non mee pee-<u>a</u>che

I like swimming/traveling
Mi piace nuotare/viaggiare
mee pee-<u>a</u>che nwot<u>a</u>re/vyaj-j<u>a</u>re

I hate …
Odio …
<u>o</u>dee-o

Do you like …?
Le piace …?
le pee-<u>a</u>che

It's delicious/awful!
È buonissimo/terribile!
eh bwon<u>ee</u>s-seemo/ter-r<u>ee</u>beele

I don't drink/smoke
Non bevo/fumo
non b<u>e</u>vo/f<u>oo</u>mo

Do you mind if I smoke?
Le dispiace se fumo?
le deespee-<u>a</u>che se f<u>oo</u>mo

I don't eat meat or fish
Non mangio nè la carne nè il pesce
non m<u>a</u>njo neh la k<u>a</u>rne neh eel p<u>e</u>she

What would you like (to drink)?
Cosa desidera (da bere)?
k<u>o</u>za dez<u>ee</u>daira da b<u>ai</u>re

I would like a ...
Vorrei un/una ...
vor-re̱ oon/o̱ona

Nothing for me, thanks
Per me niente, grazie
pair me nee-e̱nte gra̱tzee-e

I'll get this one
Prenderò questo
prendairo̱ kwe̱sto

Cheers! *(toast)*
Alla salute!/Cin cin!
a̱l-la salo̱ote/cheen cheen

I would like to ...
Vorrei ...
vor-ra̱y

Let's go to Florence/the movies/the exhibition
Andiamo a Firenze/al cinema/alla mostra
and-ya̱mo a feere̱ntze/al che̱enema/a̱l-la mo̱stra

Let's go swimming/for a walk
Andiamo a nuotare/a fare una passeggiata
and-ya̱mo a nwota̱re/a fa̱re o̱ona pas-sej-ja̱ta

What's the weather like?
Che tempo fa?
ke te̱mpo fa

The weather's awful
È brutto tempo
eh bro̱ot-to te̱mpo

It's pouring down
Sta piovendo a dirotto
sta p-yove̱ndo a deero̱t-to

It's really hot
Fa veramente caldo
fa veramente kaldo

It's sunny
C'è il sole
cheh eel sole

HELP, PROBLEMS

Can you help me?
Può aiutarmi?
pwo i-ootarmee

I don't understand
Non capisco
non kapeesko

Do you speak English/French/German?
Parla inglese/francese/tedesco?
parla eengleze/francheze/tedesko

Does anyone here speak English?
C'è qualcuno che parla inglese?
cheh kwalkoono ke parla eengleze

I can't speak Italian
Non parlo italiano
non parlo eetal-yano

I don't know
Non so
non so

What's wrong?
Cosa c'è che non va?
koza cheh ke non va

Please speak more slowly
Per favore, parli più lentamente
pair favore parlee p-yoo lentamente

Please write it down for me
Me lo scriva, per favore
me lo skreeva pair favore

I'm lost *(said by a man/woman)*
Mi sono perso/persa
mee sono pairso/pairsa

Go away! *(familiar)*
Se ne vada! Vattene!
se ne vada *vat-tene*

TALKING TO RECEPTIONISTS, ETC.

I have an appointment with ...
Ho un appuntamento con ...
o oon ap-poontamento kon

I'd like to see ...
Vorrei vedere ...
vor-ray vedaire

Here's my card
Questo è il mio biglietto da visita
kwesto eh eel mee-o beel-yet-to da veez-eeta

My company is ...
La mia società è ...
la mee-a socheta eh

May I use your phone?
Posso usare il telefono?
pos-so oozare eel telefono

THINGS YOU'LL SEE

acqua potabile	drinking water
affittasi	to rent
aperto	open
ascensore	elevator
buffet	snack bar
cassa	cash register
chiuso	closed
chiuso per ferie	closed for vacation
entrata	entrance
entrata libera	free admission
feriali	working days
festivi	national holidays
gabinetti	restroom
libero	vacant, free
occupato	occupied
orario di apertura	opening hours
orario di visita	visiting hours
piano terra	ground floor
primo piano	second floor
riservato	reserved
saldi/sconti	sales
servizi	restroom
signore	women
signori	men
si prega di non ...	please do not ...
spingere	push
strada	road
svendita	sale
tirare	pull
ufficio informazioni	tourist information
uscita	exit
uscita di sicurezza	emergency exit
vendesi	for sale
vernice fresca	wet paint

→

via	street
vietato	forbidden
vietato l'ingresso	no entrance

THINGS YOU'LL HEAR

a più tardi	see you later
arrivederci	goodbye
attenzione!	look out! pay attention!
avanti!	come in!
bene	good, fine
buon viaggio!	have a good trip!
come stai/sta/state?	how are you?
come va?	how are things?
cosa hai/ha detto?	what did you say?
davvero?	really?
ecco-ti qua!	here you are!
esattamente	exactly
grazie	thanks
grazie, anche a lei	thank you, the same to you
mi dispiace tanto!	I'm so sorry!
mi scusi	excuse me
molte grazie	thank you very much
molto bene, grazie	very well, thank you
—e lei?	—and you?
non capisco	I don't understand
non so	I don't know
prego	you're welcome, don't mention it
prego?	excuse me?
serviti/si serva/servitevi	help yourself
scusi?, come?	excuse me?
si	yes
va bene	that's right

COLLOQUIALISMS

You may hear these. To use some of them yourself could be risky!

accidenti!	damn!
che schifo!	it's disgusting!
chiudi il becco!	shut up!
cretino	idiot, fool
Dio mio!	my God!
e allora?	so what?
è orribile!	it's awful!
fa' pure!	do as you please; please, do!
grazie a Dio!	thank God!
maledetto …	damned …
maledizione!	damn!
ma va?	really?
ma va!	I don't believe it
meglio così	so much the better
muoviti!	hurry up!
non posso crederci!	I can't believe it!
occhio!	watch out!
per Dio!	by God!
porca miseria!	oh, hell!
prova!	just try!
sei pazzo?	you must be crazy!
sparisci!	scram!
stupendo!	great!
svitato	crazy, nuts
ti sta bene!	it serves you right!
tizio	guy
togliti dai piedi!	get out of the way!
va al diavolo!/va all'inferno!	go to hell!
va a quel paese!	get lost!
va bene!	that's fine; it's OK!
zitto!	shut up!

DAYS, MONTHS, SEASONS

Sunday	domenica	*dom<u>e</u>neeka*
Monday	lunedì	*loon<u>ed</u>ee*
Tuesday	martedì	*mart<u>ed</u>ee*
Wednesday	mercoledì	*mairkol<u>ed</u>ee*
Thursday	giovedì	*jov<u>ed</u>ee*
Friday	venerdì	*venaird<u>ee</u>*
Saturday	sabato	*s<u>a</u>bato*

January	gennaio	*jen-n<u>a</u>-yo*
February	febbraio	*feb-br<u>a</u>-yo*
March	marzo	*m<u>a</u>rtzo*
April	aprile	*apr<u>ee</u>le*
May	maggio	*m<u>aj</u>-jo*
June	giugno	*j<u>oo</u>n-yo*
July	luglio	*l<u>ool</u>-yo*
August	agosto	*ag<u>o</u>sto*
September	settembre	*set-t<u>e</u>mbre*
October	ottobre	*ot-t<u>o</u>bre*
November	novembre	*nov<u>e</u>mbre*
December	dicembre	*deech<u>e</u>mbre*

Spring	primavera	*preemav<u>ai</u>ra*
Summer	estate	*est<u>a</u>te*
Fall	autunno	*owt<u>oo</u>n-no*
Winter	inverno	*eenv<u>ai</u>rno*

Christmas	Natale	*nat<u>a</u>le*
Christmas Eve	la Vigilia di Natale	*veej<u>eel</u>-ya dee nat<u>a</u>le*
Good Friday	Venerdì Santo	*venaird<u>ee</u> s<u>a</u>nto*
Easter	Pasqua	*p<u>a</u>skwa*
New Year	Capodanno	*kapod<u>a</u>n-no*
New Year's Eve	San Silvestro	*san seelv<u>e</u>stro*
Pentecost	Pentecoste	*pentek<u>o</u>ste*

NUMBERS

0	zero *tzairo*	10	dieci *dee-echee*
1	uno *oono*	11	undici *oon-deechee*
2	due *doo-e*	12	dodici *doh-deechee*
3	tre *tre*	13	tredici *tre-deechee*
4	quattro *kwat-tro*	14	quattordici *kwat-tor-deechee*
5	cinque *cheenkwe*	15	quindici *kween-deechee*
6	sei *say*	16	sedici *say-deechee*
7	sette *set-te*	17	diciassette *deechas-set-te*
8	otto *ot-to*	18	diciotto *deechot-to*
9	nove *no-ve*	19	diciannove *deechan-no-ve*

20 venti *ventee*
21 ventuno *vent-oono*
22 ventidue *ventee-doo-e*
30 trenta *trenta*
31 trentuno *trentoono*
32 trentadue *trentadoo-e*
40 quaranta *kwaranta*
50 cinquanta *cheenkwanta*
60 sessanta *ses-santa*
70 settanta *set-tanta*
80 ottanta *ot-tanta*
90 novanta *novanta*
100 cento *chento*
110 centodieci *chento-dee-echee*
200 duecento *doo-e-chento*
1,000 mille *meele*
10,000 diecimila *dee-echeemeela*
20,000 ventimila *venteemeela*
50,000 cinquantamila *cheenkwantameela*
54,250 cinquantaquattromila duecentocinquanta *cheenkwanta-kwat-tro-meela doo-e-chento-cheenkwanta*
100,000 centomila *chentomeela*
1,000,000 un milione *oon meel-yone*

Note that thousands are written 1.000, 10.000, etc., in Italian.

TIME

today	oggi	*oj-jee*
yesterday	ieri	*yairee*
tomorrow	domani	*domanee*
the day before yesterday	l'altro ieri	*laltro yairee*
the day after tomorrow	dopodomani	*dopodomanee*
this week	questa settimana	*kwesta set-teemana*
last week	la settimana scorsa	*set-teemana skorsa*
next week	la settimana prossima	*set-teemana pros-seema*
this morning	stamattina	*stamat-teena*
this afternoon	questo pomeriggio	*kwesto pomereej-jo*
this evening	stasera	*stasaira*
tonight	stanotte	*stanot-te*
yesterday afternoon	ieri pomeriggio	*yairee pomereej-jo*
last night	ieri sera,	*yairee saira,*
	ieri notte	*yairee not-te*
tomorrow morning	domani mattina	*domanee mat-teena*
tomorrow night	domani sera	*domanee saira*
in three days	tra tre giorni	*tra tre jornee*
three days ago	tre giorni fa	*tre jornee fa*
late	tardi	*tardee*
early	presto	*presto*
soon	presto	*presto*
later on	più tardi	*p-yoo tardee*
at the moment	in questo momento	*een kwesto momento*
second	un secondo	*sekondo*
minute	un minuto	*meenooto*
two minutes	due minuti	*doo-e meenootee*
quarter of an hour	un quarto d'ora	*kwarto dora*
half an hour	mezz'ora	*medzora*
three quarters of an hour	tre quarti d'ora	*tre kwartee dora*

hour	un'ora	_ora_
day	un giorno	_jorno_
week	una settimana	_set-teemana_
two weeks	quindici giorni	_kween-deechee jornee_
month	un mese	_meze_
year	un anno	_an-no_
that day	quel giorno	_kwel jorno_
every day	ogni giorno	_on-yee jorno_
all day	tutto il giorno	_toot-to eel jorno_
the next day	il giorno dopo	_jorno dopo_

TELLING TIME

The hour is expressed in Italian by the ordinal number only:
sono le due "it's two o'clock," **alle due** "at two o'clock." There
is no equivalent of "o'clock." To denote the half hour, add
e mezza after the hour: **sono le due e mezza** "it's 2:30." To say
"quarter past," add **e un quarto** "and a quarter" to the hour:
sono le tre e un quarto is "it's a quarter past three."

Quarter to the hour is expressed either by adding **e tre quarti**
"and three quarters" to the hour, or adding **meno un quarto**
"less a quarter" to the next hour. "It's a quarter to eight" is
therefore **sono le sette e tre quarti** *or* **sono le otto meno
un quarto.**

To express minutes past the hour, add the minutes to the hour:
sono le sette e quaranta "it's seven forty." Minutes to the hour are
expressed by adding **meno** followed by the number of minutes
to the next hour: **sono le otto meno venti** "it's twenty to eight."

There are no equivalents of AM and PM in Italian, although
you could use **di mattina/del mattino** "in the morning," **di/del
pomeriggio** "in the afternoon," **di sera** "in the evening," and
di notte "at night." For example, "10 AM" is **le dieci di mattina/
del mattino**; "6 PM" is **le sei di/del pomeriggio**; "10 PM" is
le dieci di sera; "2 AM" is **le due di notte** (but also **le due
del mattino**).

The 24-hour clock is also used, both in the written form as in timetables, and verbally as in inquiry offices and when making appointments.

what time is it?	che ore sono?	*ke ore sono?*
it's one o'clock	è l'una	*eh loona*
it's two/three/four o'clock	sono le due/tre/ quattro	*sono le doo-e/tre/ kwat-tro*
ten past one	l'una e dieci	*loona ay dee-echee*
quarter past one	l'una e un quarto	*loona ay oon kwarto*
1:30	l'una e mezza	*loona ay medza*
twenty to two	le due meno venti	*lay doo-e meno ventee*
quarter to two	le due meno un quarto	*le doo-e meno oon kwarto*
two o'clock	le due	*le doo-e*
13:00	le tredici	*le tre-deechee*
16:30	le sedici e trenta	*le se-deechee ay trenta*
at 5:30	alle cinque e mezza	*al-le cheenkwe ay medza*
at seven o'clock	alle sette	*al-le set-te*
noon	mezzogiorno	*medzojorno*
midnight	mezzanotte	*medzanot-te*

THE CALENDAR

The cardinal numbers on page 19 are used to express the date in Italian, except for the first when the ordinal **il primo** is used:

May first	il primo maggio	*eel preemo maj-jo*
September second	il due settembre	*eel doo-e set-tembre*
June twentieth	il venti giugno	*eel ventee joon-yo*

HOTELS

Hotels in Italy are classified according to the familiar star system: one, two, three, four, and five stars. At the bottom of the range you'll find **locande** (one-star hotels) and **pensioni** (one- or two-star hotels). The prices are displayed in the rooms and they do not always include breakfast, but should include service charges and taxes.

In some areas, the local **APT** (**Azienda di Promozione Turistica**) can supply information about hotels, but in others tourism is coordinated by an **AAST** (**Azienda Autonoma di Soggiorno e Turismo**). It is also possible to obtain a list of hotels from information offices in stations and airports. If you arrive in a town without having reserved beforehand, go directly to the **APT** or to the **AAST** for help. Leaflets will be available in English, and usually at least one person there will speak English.

Hotel breakfasts consist mainly of a **brioche** (a type of croissant) or bread, butter and jam, and coffee or tea. Some hotels may provide a full breakfast on request.

USEFUL WORDS AND PHRASES

balcony	il balcone	*bal-kone*
bath (*tub*)	la vasca da bagno	*vaska da ban-yo*
bathroom	il bagno	*ban-yo*
bed	il letto	*let-to*
bed and breakfast	camera con colazione	*kamaira kon kolatz-yone*
bed and breakfast hotel	la pensione familiare	*penz-yone fameel-yare*
bedroom	la camera da letto	*kamaira da let-to*
bill	il conto	*konto*
breakfast	la prima colazione	*preema kolatz-yone*
dining room	la sala da pranzo	*sala da prantzo*
dinner	la cena	*chena*

double bed	il letto matrimoniale	*let-to matreemonyale*
double room	la stanza doppia	*stantza doppee-a*
elevator	l'ascensore	*ashen-sore*
foyer	la hall	*oll*
full board	la pensione completa	*pens-yone kompleta*
guesthouse	la pensione, la locanda	*pens-yone, lokanda*
half board	la mezza pensione	*medza pens-yone,*
hotel	l'albergo, l'hotel	*albairgo, oh-tel*
key	la chiave	*k-yave*
lounge	il salone	*salone*
lunch	il pranzo, la seconda colazione	*prantzo, sekonda kolatz-yone*
maid	la cameriera	*kamair-yaira*
manager	il direttore	*deeret-tore*
parking lot	il parcheggio	*parkej-jo*
receipt	la ricevuta	*reechevoota*
reception	la reception	*'reception'*
receptionist	il/la receptionist	*'receptionist'*
restaurant	il ristorante	*reestorante*
room	la camera, la stanza	*kamaira, stantza*
room service	il servizio in camera	*serveetz-yo een kamaira*
shower	la doccia	*docha*
single bed	il letto singolo	*let-to seengolo*
single room	la stanza singola	*stantza seengola*
sink	il lavandino	*lavandeeno*
toilet	la toilette	*twalet*
twin room	la stanza con due letti	*stantza kon doo-e lettee*

Do you have any vacancies?
Avete una stanza libera?
avete oona stantza leebaira

I have a reservation
Ho prenotato una stanza
o prenotato oona stantza

I'd like a single room
Vorrei una stanza singola
vor-ray oona stantza seengola

I'd like a room with a bathroom/balcony
Vorrei una stanza con bagno/con il balcone
vor-ray oona stantza kon ban-yo/kon eel bal-kone

Is there satellite/cable TV in the rooms?
C'è la TV satellite/cavo in queste stanze?
Cheh la tee-vee satail-lee-te/kavo een kwaiste stantze

I'd like a room for one night/three nights
Vorrei una stanza per una notte/tre notti
vor-ray oona stantza pair oona not-te/tre not-tee

What is the charge per night?
Quanto si paga per notte?
kwanto see paga pair not-te

I don't yet know how long I'll stay
Non so ancora quanto tempo rimarrò
non so ankora kwanto tempo reemarro

When is breakfast/dinner?
A che ora viene servita la colazione/la cena?
a ke ora v-yene serveeta la kolatz-yone/la chena

Please wake me at … o'clock
Mi svegli, per favore, alle …
mee zvel-yee pair favore al-le …

May I have breakfast in my room?
Potrei avere la colazione in camera?
potray avaire la kolatz-yone een kamaira

I'd like to have some laundry done
Vorrei far pulire alcuni indumenti
vor-ray far pooleere alkoonee eendoomentee

I'll be back at … o'clock
Tornerò alle …
tornairo al-le …

My room number is …
Il mio numero di stanza è …
eel mee-o noomero dee stantza eh …

My reservation was for a double room
Avevo prenotato una stanza doppia
avevo prenotato oona stantza dop-pia

I asked for a room with a private bathroom
Avevo chiesto una stanza con bagno
avevo k-yesto oona stantza kon ban-yo

There is no toilet paper in the bathroom
Non c'è carta igienica in bagno
non cheh karta eej-yeneeka een ban-yo

The window won't open
La finestra non si apre
la feenestra non see apre

The elevator/shower isn't working
L'ascensore/la doccia non funziona
lashen-sore/la docha non foontz-yona

There isn't any hot water
Non c'è acqua calda
non cheh akwa kalda

The outlet in the bathroom doesn't work
La presa di corrente del bagno non funziona
la preza dee kor-rente del ban-yo non foontz-yona

I'm leaving tomorrow
Parto domani
parto domanee

When do I have to vacate the room?
Entro che ora devo liberare la camera?
entro ke ora devo leebairare la kamaira

Can I have the bill, please?
Mi da il conto, per favore?
mee da eel konto pair favore

I'll pay by credit card
Pago con la carta di credito
pago kon la karta dee kredeeto

I'll pay cash
Pago in contanti
pago een kontantee

Can you get me a taxi, please?
Potrebbe chiamarmi un taxi, per favore?
potreb-be k-yamarmee oon 'taxi' pair favore

Can you recommend another hotel?
Potrebbe consigliarmi un altro albergo?
potreb-be konseel-yarmee oon altro albairgo

THINGS YOU'LL SEE

albergo	hotel
ascensore	elevator
bagno	bathroom
camera con prima colazione	bed and breakfast
cena	dinner
chiave	key
colazione	breakfast
completo	no vacancies

→

conto	bill
entrata	entrance
locanda	guesthouse
mezza pensione	half board
parcheggio	parking lot
parcheggio riservato agli ospiti dell'albergo	parking reserved for hotel patrons only
pensione	guesthouse
pensione completa	full board
pianterreno	ground floor
pranzo	lunch
prenotazione	reservation
primo piano	second floor
scale	stairs
spingere	push
tirare	pull
uscita d'emergenza	emergency exit

THINGS YOU'LL HEAR

Mi spiace, siamo al completo
I'm sorry, we're full

Non ci sono più camere singole/doppie
There are no single/double rooms left

Per quante notti?
For how many nights?

Come vuole pagare?
How will you be paying?

Pagamento anticipato, per favore
Please pay in advance

Dovete liberare la stanza entro mezzogiorno
You must vacate the room by noon

CAMPING AND TRAILER TRAVEL

Campsites in Italy usually have excellent facilities. Prices differ according to the size of the tent (**casetta** = little house, **canadese** = two-person tent) and/or the number of people sharing it. You can generally pay for a parking space next to the tent. Moving the car at certain times—mealtimes, for example—is forbidden because it raises dust. If you go out in the evening, you will not be allowed to bring your car back inside the site after midnight, but there are often parking facilities just outside.

Most campsites have electric generators. A small daily fee will be added to your bill if you use them. Toilet and bathing facilities are generally very good. You may have to pay for a hot shower with coins or tokens, that you insert into a machine attached to the shower. If tokens (**gettoni**) are needed, these will be available at the campsite office. Cold showers are free. The campsite office usually acts as a mini-bank as well. You can deposit all your money there and withdraw it on a daily basis. The office will also exchange foreign currency.

USEFUL WORDS AND PHRASES

backpack	lo zaino	*tza-eeno*
bonfire	il falò	*falo*
bucket	il secchio	*sek-yo*
camper (RV)	la roulotte	*roolot*
camper (RV) site	il campeggio	*kampej-jo*
go camping	andare in campeggio	*andare een kampej-jo*
campsite	il campeggio	*kampej-jo*
cooking utensils	gli utensili da cucina	*ootenseelee da koocheena*
drinking water	l'acqua potabile	*akwa pota-beele*
garbage	l'immondizia	*eem-mondeetzee-a*

groundcloth	il telone impermeabile	*telone eempair-me abeele*
hitchhike	fare l'autostop	*fare lowto-stop*
rope	la fune, la corda	*foone, korda*
saucepans	le pentole	*pentole*
sleeping bag	il sacco a pelo	*sak-ko a pelo*
tent	la tenda	*tenda*
tokens	i gettoni	*jet-tonee*
youth hostel	l'ostello della gioventù	*ostel-lo del-la joventoo*

Can I camp here?
Posso campeggiare qui?
pos-so kampej-jare kwee

Can we park the camper here?
Possiamo parcheggiare la roulotte qui?
poss-yamo parkej-jare la roolot kwee

Where is the nearest campsite/camper site?
Qual è il campeggio più vicino?
kwal eh eel kampej-jo p-yoo veecheeno

What is the charge per night?
Quanto si paga per notte?
kwanto see paga pair not-te

I only want to stay for one night
Vorrei fermarmi solo una notte
vor-ray fairmarmee solo oona not-te

How much is it for a week?
Quanto mi viene a costare per una settimana?
kwanto mee v-yene a kostare pair oona set-teemana

We're leaving tomorrow
Partiamo domani
part-yamo domanee

Where is the kitchen?
Dov'è la cucina?
dov<u>eh</u> la kooch<u>ee</u>na

Can I light a fire here?
Posso accendere il fuoco qui?
p<u>o</u>s-so ach<u>e</u>ndaire eel fw<u>o</u>ko kwee

Can I have some tokens for the shower?
Potrei avere alcuni gettoni per la doccia?
p<u>o</u>tray av<u>ai</u>re alk<u>oo</u>nee jet-t<u>o</u>nee pair la d<u>o</u>cha

Where can I get …?
Dove posso trovare …?
d<u>o</u>ve p<u>o</u>s-so trov<u>a</u>re

Is there any drinking water?
C'è acqua potabile?
cheh <u>a</u>kwa pot<u>a</u>-beele

THINGS YOU'LL SEE

acqua potabile	drinking water
a persona	per person
campeggio	campsite
cucina	kitchen
docce	showers
gabinetti	toilets
ostello della gioventù	youth hostel
rimorchio	trailer
roulotte	camper (RV)
tariffa	charge
tenda	tent
vietato accendere fuochi	no campfires
vietato il campeggio	no camping

VILLAS AND APARTMENTS

In Italy, you can arrange to rent an apartment through travel agencies or through a real estate agent. If you make a reservation, you will be asked to leave a deposit in advance.

When you arrive in the tourist resort where you have reserved the villa or apartment, you will have to sign a contract. Your name, the date of the rental, the address of the apartment, the amount of your deposit, etc., will be specified in this contract. You may be asked to pay for certain "extras" not included in the original price. Gas and electricity are normally included, but cleaning seldom is. It's a good idea to ask about an inventory of goods at the start, rather than be told something is missing just as you are about to leave. Sometimes you will find an inventory in the apartment (in a drawer or cabinet). Usually, you are not required to sign it.

You may be asked for a deposit, in case you break something. Make sure this is specified in the contract you sign. You will get your money back when you leave.

USEFUL WORDS AND PHRASES

English	Italian	Pronunciation
bath *(tub)*	la vasca da bagno	v<u>a</u>ska da b<u>a</u>n-yo
bathroom	il bagno	b<u>a</u>n-yo
bedroom	la camera da letto	k<u>a</u>maira da l<u>e</u>t-to
blocked	intasato	eentaz<u>a</u>to
boiler	lo scaldabagno	skaldab<u>a</u>n-yo
broken	rotto	r<u>o</u>t-to
caretaker	il portinaio	porteen<u>i</u>-o
(female)	la portinaia	porteen<u>i</u>-a
central heating	il riscaldamento centrale	reeskaldam<u>e</u>nto chentr<u>a</u>le
cleaner	l'uomo delle pulizie	w<u>o</u>mo d<u>e</u>l-le pooleetz<u>ee</u>-e
(female)	la donna delle pulizie	d<u>o</u>n-na d<u>e</u>l-le pooleetz<u>ee</u>-e

comforter	il piumino	p-yoomeeno
deposit (security)	la cauzione	kowtz-yone
(part payment)	la caparra	kapar-ra
drain	lo scarico	skareeko
electrician	l'elettricista	elet-treecheesta
electricity	l'elettricità	elet-treecheeta
faucet	il rubinetto	roobeenet-to
fusebox	la scatola dei fusibili	skatola day foozeebeelee
garbage can	il bidone della spazzatura	beedone del-la spatzzatoora
gas	il gas	'gas'
grill	la griglia	greel-ya
heater	il termosifone	tair-mo-see-fone
iron	il ferro da stiro	fair-ro da steero
ironing board	la tavola da stiro	tavola da steero
keys	le chiavi	k-ya-vee
kitchen	la cucina	koocheena
leak (noun)	la perdita	pairdeeta
(verb)	perdere	pairdaire
light	la luce	looche
living room	il soggiorno	soj-jorno
maid	la cameriera	kamair-yaira
pillow	il cuscino	koosheeno
pillowcase	la federa	fedaira
plumber	l'idraulico	eedrowleeko
real estate agent	l'agente immobiliare	ajente eem-mobeelyare
refrigerator	il frigorifero	freegoreefairo
refund	il rimborso	reemborso
sheets	le lenzuola	lentzwola
shower	la doccia	docha
sink	il lavandino	lavandeeno
stopper	il rubinetto d'arresto	roobeenet-to dar-resto
stove	il fornello	fornel-lo

swimming pool	la piscina	*peesheena*
toilet	il gabinetto	*gabeenet-to*
towel	l'asciugamano	*ashoogamano*
washing machine	la lavatrice	*lavatreeche*
water	l'acqua	*akwa*
water heater	lo scaldabagno	*skalda-ban-yo*

I'd like to rent an apartment/a villa for … days
Vorrei affittare un appartamento/una villa per … giorni
vor-ray af-feet-tare oon ap-partamento/oona veel-la pair … jornee

Do I have to pay a deposit?
Devo versare una cauzione?
devo vairsare oona kowtz-yone

Does the price include gas and electricity?
Il gas e l'elettricità sono inclusi nel prezzo?
eel 'gas' ay lelet-treecheeta sono eenkloozee nel pretzo

Where is this item?
Dove si trova questo oggetto?
dove see trova kwesto oj-jet-to

Please take it off the inventory
Lo tolga dall'inventario, per favore
lo tolga dal-leenventar-yo pair favore

We've broken this
Abbiamo rotto questo
abb-yamo rot-to kwesto

This was broken when we arrived
Era già rotto quando siamo arrivati
era ja rot-to kwando s-yamo ar-reevatee

This was missing when we arrived
Non c'era quando siamo arrivati
non chera kwando s-yamo ar-reevatee

Can I have my deposit back?
Potrei riavere la cauzione?
potray ree-avaire la kowtz-yone

Can we have an extra bed?
Potremmo avere un letto in più?
potrem-mo avaire oon let-to een p-yoo

Can we have more dishes/silverware?
Potremmo avere ancora un po' di stoviglie/posate?
potrem-mo avaire ankora oon po dee stoveel-ye/pozate

When does the maid come?
Quando viene la cameriera?
kwando v-yene la kamair-yaira

Where can I buy/find ...?
Dove posso comprare/trovare ...?
dove pos-so komprare/trovare

How does the water heater work?
Come funziona lo scaldabagno?
kome foontz-yona lo skalda-ban-yo

Do you do ironing/baby-sitting?
Sa stirare/badare ai bambini?
sa steerare/badare i bambeenee

Do you prepare lunch/dinner?
È in grado di preparare il pranzo/la cena?
eh een grado dee preparare eel prantzo/la chena

Do we have to pay extra or is it included?
Dobbiamo pagarlo a parte o è incluso nel prezzo?
dobb-yamo pagarlo a parte o eh eenkloozo nel pret-zo

The shower doesn't work
La doccia non funziona
la docha non foontz-yona

The sink is blocked
Il lavandino è intasato
eel lavandeeno eh eentazato

The sink/toilet is leaking
Il lavandino/gabinetto perde
eel lavandeeno/gabeenet-to pairde

There's a burst pipe
Si è rotto un tubo
see eh rot-to oon toobo

The garbage has not been collected for a week
Non portano via la spazzatura da una settimana
non portano vee-a la spatz-zatoora da oona set-teemana

There's no electricity/gas/water
Non c'è elettricità/gas/acqua
non cheh elet-treecheeta/'gas'/akwa

Can you fix it today?
Può ripararlo oggi?
pwo reepararlo oj-jee

Send your bill to …
Mandi il conto a …
mandee eel konto a

I'm staying at …
Sto a …
sto a

Thank you for everything!
Grazie di tutto!
gratzee-e dee toot-to

See you again next year!
Al prossimo anno!
al pros-seemo an-no

DRIVING

In Italy you drive on the right and pass on the left. On divided highways you may stay in the left-hand lane if heavy traffic has taken over the right-hand lane. Normally, you may move from the right- to the left-hand lane only for turning or passing. On three-lane roads with traffic flowing in both directions, the central lane is for passing only.

At intersections where there are no road signs or traffic lights, you must yield to traffic coming from the right, except in the case of a service station exit, a private road, or a track entering the main road. Usually, a diamond-shaped yellow sign tells you that you have the right of way. The end of this right of way is indicated by a similar sign with a bar through it. An upside-down red triangle or a "STOP" sign means that you must yield to all vehicles coming from both the right and the left.

In built-up areas the speed limit is 31 mph (50 km/h). On open roads (if not otherwise indicated) it is 56 mph (90 km/h), and on highways it is 81 mph (130 km/h).

If you break down and are forced to stop in the middle of the road, you must place a red triangle about 160 feet (50 meters) behind your vehicle to warn other drivers. All drivers must carry this triangle, which can be rented from the offices of the **ACI** (**Automobile Club Italiano**) when you enter Italy and then returned when you leave the country.

There are emergency telephones on most highways. If you break down on the **Autostrada del Sole** (Milan–Rome) or on another main highway, there are emergency telephones on the right side of the road at intervals of 1 or 2 km. Generally, it is illegal to walk along the highway or hitchhike but, if the break-down occurs between two telephones, you are allowed to walk to the next emergency phone. (Also see Emergencies, page 107.)

Most towns have shopping centers and, if you park where you are not supposed to, your car will be towed away. You should park either in a free parking area or in a paying parking lot or garage. Charges are displayed on a sign in the parking lot.

You'll be given a parking ticket when you arrive or, if there is a parking lot attendant, he or she will place a ticket on your windshield and you pay on departure.

SOME COMMON ROAD SIGNS

accendere i fari	headlights on
attenzione	watch out, caution
autostrada	highway (with toll)
banchina non transitabile	soft shoulder
caduta massi	falling rocks
centro	town center
code	traffic ahead
controllo automatico della velocità	automatic speed monitor
cunetta o dosso	ditch
deviazione	detour
disporsi su due file	two-lane traffic
divieto di accesso	no entry
divieto di fermata	no stopping
divieto di transito	no thoroughfare
dogana	customs
escluso residenti	residents only
fine del tratto autostradale	end of highway
ghiaccio	ice
incrocio	junction
incrocio pericoloso	dangerous junction/ intersection
informazioni turistiche	tourist information
lavori in corso	construction site
nebbia	fog
non oltrepassare	no trespassing
pagare qui	pay here
parcheggio a giorni alterni	parking on alternate days
parcheggio a pagamento	paying parking lot

→

parcheggio custodito	parking lot with attendant
parcheggio incustodito	unattended parking lot
pedaggio	toll
pedoni	pedestrians
pericolo	danger
pista ciclabile	bicycle trail
rallentare	reduce speed
scuola	school
senso unico	one way
sosta vietata	no parking
sottopassaggio	subway
strada a fondo cieco	dead end
strada camionabile	route for heavy vehicles
strada ghiacciata	ice on road
strada statale	main road
strada sdrucciolevole	slippery road
strada secondaria	secondary road
strada statale	main road
uscita camion	construction exit
veicoli lenti	slow lane
zona a traffico limitato	restricted traffic area
zona pedonale	shopping center

USEFUL WORDS AND PHRASES

automatic	con il cambio automatico	*kon eel kam-bee-o owtomateeko*
beltway	raccordo anulare	*rak-kordo anoolare*
brake	il freno	*freno*
breakdown	il guasto	*gwasto*
car	l'automobile, la macchina	*owtomobeele, mak-keena*
car ferry	il traghetto	*traget-to*
clutch	la frizione	*freetz-yone*
drive	guidare	*gweedare*
engine	il motore	*motore*

exhaust	lo scappamento	*skap-pamento*
fanbelt	la cinghia della ventola	*cheeng-ya del-la ventola*
garage *(for repairs)*	l'autorimessa	*owtoreemes-sa*
gas	la benzina	*bendzeena*
gas station	la stazione di servizio	*statz-yone dee sairveetz-yo*
gear	il cambio, la marcia	*kam-bee-o, marcha*
gears	le marce	*marche*
headlights	i fari	*faree*
highway	l'autostrada	*owtostrada*
hood	il cofano	*kofano*
intersection	l'incrocio	*eenkrocho*
junction	l'incrocio	*eenkrocho*
(highway entry)	raccordo di entrata	*rak-kordo dee entrata*
(highway exit)	raccordo di uscita	*rak-kordo dee oosheeta*
license	la patente	*patente*
license plate	la targa	*targa*
manual	con il cambio manuale	*kon eel kam-bee-o manwale*
mirror	lo specchietto	*spekk-yet-to*
motorcycle	la motocicletta	*motocheeklet-ta*
parking lot	il parcheggio	*parkej-jo*
road	la strada	*strada*
spare parts	i pezzi di ricambio	*petzee dee reekam-bee-o*
spark plug	la candela	*kandela*
speed	la velocità	*velocheeta*
speed limit	il limite di velocità	*leemeete dee velocheeta*
speedometer	il tachimetro	*takeemetro*
steering wheel	il volante	*volante*
taillights	i fari posteriori	*faree postair-yoree*

tire	la gomma	*gom-ma*
traffic lights	il semaforo	*semaforo*
trailer	il rimorchio,	*reemork-yo,*
	la roulotte	*roolot*
transmission	la scatola del cambio	*skatola dek kam-bee-o*
truck	il camion,	*kam-yon,*
	l'autocarro	*owtokar-ro*
trunk	il portabagagli	*portabagal-yee*
turn signal	la freccia	*frech-cha*
van	il furgone	*foorgone*
warning sign	il triangolo	*tree-angolo*
wheel	la ruota	*rwota*
windshield	il parabrezza	*parabretza*
windshield wiper	il tergicristallo	*tairjee-kreestal-lo*

Could you check the oil/water level, please?
Potrebbe controllare il livello dell'olio/dell'acqua, per favore?
potreb-be kontrol-lare eel leevel-lo del ol-yo/del akwa pair favore

Fill it up, please!
Faccia il pieno, per favore
facha eel p-yeno pair favore

I'd like 35 liters of leaded gas, please
Mi dia trentacinque litri di super, per favore
mee dee-a trentacheenkwe leetree dee soopair pair favore

Do you do repairs?
Effettua riparazioni?
ef-fet-too-a reeparatz-yonee

Can you repair the clutch?
Può ripararmi la frizione?
pwo reepararmee la freetz-yone

There is something wrong with the engine
C'è qualcosa che non va nel motore
cheh kwalkoza ke non va nel motore

The engine is overheating
Il motore si surriscalda
eel motore see soor-reeskalda

I need a new tire
Ho bisogno di una gomma nuova
o beezon-yo dee oona gom-ma nwova

Can you replace this?
Può sostituirlo?
pwo sosteetoo-eerlo

The turn signal is not working
La freccia non funziona
la frech-cha non foontz-yona

How long will it take?
Quanto tempo ci vorrà?
kwanto tempo chee vor-ra

Where can I park?
Dove posso parcheggiare?
dove pos-so parkej-jare

I'd like to rent a car
Vorrei noleggiare una macchina
vor-ray nolej-jare oona mak-keena

I'd like an automatic/a manual
Vorrei una macchina con il cambio automatico/manuale
vor-ray oona mak-keena kon eel kam-bee-o owtomateeko/manwale

How much is it for one day?
Quanto costa per un giorno?
kwanto kosta pair oon jorno

Is there a mileage charge?
C'è un supplemento per il chilometraggio?
cheh oon soop-plemento pair eel keelometraj-jo

When do I have to return it?
Quando devo riportarla?
kwando devo reeportarla

Where is the nearest gas station?
Dov'è la stazione di servizio più vicina?
doveh la statz-yone dee sairveetz-yo p-yoo veecheena

How do I get to …?
Può dirmi come andare a …?
pwo deermee kome andare a

Is this the road to …?
È questa la strada per …?
eh kwesta la strada pair

Which is the quickest way to …?
Qual è la strada più breve per …?
kwal eh la strada p-yoo breve pair

THINGS YOU'LL SEE

acqua	water
area di servizio	service area
aspirapolvere	vacuum cleaner
autolavaggio	car wash
autorimessa	garage (for repairs)
benzina	gas
benzina senza piombo	unleaded gas
benzina super	leaded gas
casello autostradale	highway toll booth
cera per auto	car wax
code	line of traffic
deviazione	detour
gasolio	diesel oil
gommista	tire repairs
guidare a passo d'uomo	drive at walking speed

→

liquido tergicristallo	windshield wiper fluid
olio	oil
raccordo autostradale	highway junction
spegnere il motore	turn off engine
spingere	push
stazione di servizio	service station
tirare	pull
uscita	exit
vietato fumare	no smoking

THINGS YOU'LL HEAR

Vuole una macchina con il cambio automatico o manuale?
Would you like an automatic or a manual?

Esibisca la patente, per favore
May I see your license, please?

Mi fa vedere il passaporto, per favore?
May I see your passport, please?

DIRECTIONS YOU MAY BE GIVEN

a destra	right
a sinistra	left
dritto	straight ahead
giri a destra	turn right
giri a sinistra	turn left
il primo/la prima a destra	first on the right
il secondo/la seconda a sinistra	second on the left
vada oltre …	go past the …

TRAVELING AROUND

Train Travel

Train travel is so inexpensive in Italy that it is very widely used. During the holiday season, traveling by train can be difficult, so, wherever possible, you should reserve your seat well in advance. Children under four years of age not occupying a seat travel free, and there is a half-price fare for children between four and twelve years old. Considerable reductions are available for families and individuals on short-term season tickets. Sleeper cars are available on most domestic long-distance night services, and most long-distance trains have dining cars. On shorter trips there will be a cart from which you can buy sandwiches and soft drinks. In main stations, platform vendors pass by the train windows.

Trains on Italian State Railways (**Ferrovie dello Stato** or **FS**) are classified as follows:

EC (**Eurocity**): very fast international train, with first and second class compartments. A supplement must be paid in advance, but there is no charge for reserving a seat in advance.
IC (**Intercity**): very fast national train. Most **IC**s have first and second classes, but there are still a few with first class only. It's best to check this before departure. A supplement must be paid in advance, but reserving a seat is free.
Espresso: long-distance fast train. No supplement required.
Diretto: long-distance train stopping at main stations.
Regionale: small local train stopping at nearly every station.

You should find out in advance whether you will be taking an **IC** or **EC** train and ask to pay the supplement when you buy your ticket. If you have a round trip-ticket, you should validate it by stamping the date on both the outward bound and return parts on the day you travel. In most stations, there are ticket-stamping machines but, in small stations, you should go to the ticket office.

LONG-DISTANCE BUS TRAVEL

People do travel long distances by bus in Italy, but trains are
less expensive and quicker. Local buses for small towns and
places of interest are generally inexpensive and run frequently.
The long-distance buses often have a system similar to that of
local buses: when you enter, you stamp your ticket in the
ticket-stamping machine.

LOCAL PUBLIC TRANSPORTATION

In large cities there are several types of public transportation:
bus, trolley bus (**filobus**), tram, and subway (**Metropolitana**).
In some cities there is an integrated public transportation system,
which means that the same tickets can be used on all types of
transportation. Tickets are inexpensive and operate on a flat-
fare basis. In most cities, they are valid for 60 to 75 minutes,
but in some they are only valid for a one-way trip. Tickets can
be bought in the subway, at any newspaper kiosk, **tabaccaio**, or
ordinary bar with a "**vendita biglietti**" sign in the window.

When you enter a bus, **filobus**, etc., you must insert your
ticket into a machine that stamps the time on it. The only
restriction is that you cannot re-enter the **Metropolitana** with
the same ticket, even if you have not yet used up your 75
minutes. There are inspectors who make random checks and,
if you are traveling without a valid ticket, you can expect an
on-the-spot fine of about 25 euros. In most places, public
transportation is quick and efficient. Smoking is forbidden on
all local public transportation.

TAXI AND BOAT

It is not advisable to travel in a taxi that does not have the "taxi"
sign on top. Taxis without this sign are private taxis and may
charge astronomical prices. The marked taxis are reliable and
efficient, but they do have a high minimum charge. There is also
an extra charge for each item of luggage and for rides at night.
In Venice (where, of course, there are no buses, etc.) you travel

by **vaporetto**, a small passenger boat. You must buy your ticket in advance from the kiosk at **vaporetti** stops. There is a flat fare for all destinations. However, there are special offers such as 24-hour tickets with which you can travel on any number of boats for any distance, starting from the time when you stamp your ticket at the boat stop (not from when you buy it).

USEFUL WORDS AND PHRASES

adult	l'adulto	_adoolto_
airport	l'aeroporto	_a-airoporto_
airport shuttle	l'autobus per l'aeroporto	_owtoboos pair la-airoporto_
aisle seat	il posto vicino al corridoio	_posto veecheeno al kor-reedo-yo_
baggage claim	il ritiro bagagli	_reeteero bagal-yee_
berth (on a boat)	la cuccetta	_kooch-chet-ta_
boarding pass	la carta d'imbarco	_karta deembarko_
boat	la barca, il battello	_barka, bat-telo_
booking office	la biglietteria	_beel-yet-teree-a_
buffet	il buffet	_boofe_
bus	l'autobus	_owtoboos_
(long-distance)	la corriera	_kor-ree-aira_
bus station	la stazione degli autobus	_statz-yone del-yee owtoboos_
bus stop	la fermata dell'autobus	_fermata del lowtoboos_
carry-on luggage	il bagaglio a mano	_bagal-yo a mano_
check-in desk	l'accettazione (bagagli)	_achet-tatz-yone bagal-yee_
child	il bambino	_bambeeno_
(female)	la bambina	_bambeena_
compartment	lo scompartimento	_skomparteemento_
connection	la coincidenza	_ko-eencheedentza_
cruise	la crociera	_krochaira_

customs	la dogana	*dogana*
departure lounge	la sala d'attesa	*sala dat-teza*
dining car	il vagone ristorante	*vagone reestorante*
domestic	nazionale	*natz-yonale*
emergency exit	l'uscita di sicurezza	*oosheeta dee seekooretza*
entrance	l'entrata	*entrata*
exit	l'uscita	*oosheeta*
fare	la tariffa	*tareef-fa*
ferry	il traghetto	*trag-et-to*
first class	la prima classe	*preema klas-se*
flight	il volo	*volo*
flight number	il numero del volo	*noomairo del volo*
gate	l'uscita	*oosheeta*
international	internazionale	*eentairnatz-yonale*
lost and found	l'ufficio oggetti smarriti	*oof-feecho ojet-tee zmar-reetee*
luggage cart	il carrello	*kar-rel-lo*
luggage room	il deposito bagagli	*depozeeto bagal-yee*
nonsmoking	non fumatori	*non foomatoree*
number 5 bus	l'autobus numero cinque	*owtoboos noomero cheenkwe*
one-way ticket	il biglietto di sola andata	*beel-yet-to dee sola andata*
passport	il passaporto	*pas-saporto*
platform	il binario	*beenaree-o*
railroad	la ferrovia	*fer-rovee-a*
reserved seat	il posto riservato	*posto ree-sairvato*
round-trip ticket	il biglietto di andata e ritorno	*beel-yet-to dee andata ay reetorno*
seat	il posto	*posto*
second class	la seconda classe	*sekonda klas-se*
sleeper car	il vagone letto	*vagone let-to*
smoking	fumatori	*foomatoree*
station	la stazione	*statz-yone*
subway	la metropolitana	*metro-poleetana*

taxi	il taxi	*'taxi'*
terminal	il capolinea	*kapol<u>ee</u>ne-a*
ticket	il biglietto	*beel-y<u>e</u>t-to*
timetable	l'orario	*or<u>a</u>r-yo*
train	il treno	*tr<u>e</u>no*
tram	il tram	*'tram'*
transit system	la piantina dei	*p-yant<u>ee</u>na day tras-*
map	trasporti pubblici	*p<u>o</u>rtee p<u>oo</u>b-bleechee*
trolley bus	il filobus	*f<u>ee</u>loboos*
underground passage	il sottopassaggio	*sot-topas-s<u>aj</u>-jo*
waiting room	la sala d'attesa	*sala dat-t<u>e</u>za*
window seat	il posto vicino al	*p<u>o</u>sto veech<u>ee</u>no al*
	finestrino	*feenestr<u>ee</u>no*

AIR TRAVEL

I'd like a nonsmoking seat, please
Vorrei un posto per non fumatori, per favore
vor-r<u>ay</u> oon p<u>o</u>sto pair non foomat<u>o</u>ree pair fav<u>o</u>re

I'd like a window seat, please
Vorrei un posto vicino al finestrino
vor-r<u>ay</u> oon p<u>o</u>sto veech<u>ee</u>no al feenestr<u>ee</u>no

How long will the flight be delayed?
Con quanto ritardo partirà il volo?
kon kw<u>a</u>nto reet<u>a</u>rdo parteer<u>a</u> eel v<u>o</u>lo

Which gate for the flight to ...?
Qual è l'uscita del volo per ...?
kw<u>a</u>l eh loosh<u>ee</u>ta del v<u>o</u>lo pair

TRAIN AND BUS TRAVEL

When does the train/bus for Florence leave?
A che ora parte il treno/l'autobus per Firenze?
a ke <u>o</u>ra p<u>a</u>rte eel tr<u>e</u>no/l<u>ow</u>toboos pair feer<u>e</u>ntze

When does the train/bus from Rome arrive?
A che ora arriva il treno/l'autobus da Roma?
a ke ora ar-reeva eel treno/lowtoboos da roma

When is the next train/bus to Venice?
A che ora c'è il prossimo treno/autobus per Venezia?
a ke ora cheh eel pros-seemo treno/owtoboos pair venetzee-a

When is the first/last train/bus to Turin?
A che ora c'è il primo/l'ultimo treno/autobus per Torino?
a ke ora cheh eel preemo/loolteemo treno/owtoboos pair toreeno

What is the fare to Naples?
Quanto costa il biglietto per Napoli?
kwanto kosta eel beel-yet-to pair napolee

Do I have to change?
Devo cambiare?
devo kamb-yare

Does the train/bus stop at Padua?
Il treno/l'autobus ferma a Padova?
eel treno/lowtoboos fairma a padova

How long does it take to get to Trieste?
Quanto tempo ci mette per arrivare a Trieste?
kwanto tempo chee met-te pair ar-ree-varai a tree-este

Where can I buy a ticket?
Dove posso comprare il biglietto?
dove pos-so komprare eel beel-yet-to

A one-way/round-trip ticket to Bologna, please
Un biglietto di sola andata/di andata e ritorno per Bologna, per favore
oon beel-yet-to dee sola andata/dee andata ay reetorno pair bolon-ya pair favore

Could you help me get a ticket?
Potrebbe aiutarmi a comprare il biglietto?
potreb-be i-ootarmee a comp-rarai eel beel-yet-to

Do I have to pay a supplement?
Devo pagare un supplemento?
devo pagare oon soop-plemento

Is there a discount for children?
Fate prezzi ridotti per i bambini?
fatai pretzee ree-olot-tee pair ee bambee-nee

Do we have to pay for the children?
Si paga anche per i bambini?
see paga ankei pair ee bambee-nee

I'd like to reserve a seat
Vorrei prenotare un posto a sedere
vor-ray prenotare oon posto a sedere

Is this the right train/bus for Genoa?
È questo il treno/l'autobus per Genova?
eh kwesto eel treno/lowtoboos pair jenova

Is this the right platform for the Palermo train?
È questo il binario del treno per Palermo?
eh kwesto eel beenaree-o del treno pair palairmo

Which platform for the Perugia train?
Da che binario parte il treno per Perugia?
da ke beenaree-o parte eel treno pair perooja

Is the train/bus late?
Il treno/l'autobus è in ritardo?
eel treno/lowtoboos eh een reetardo

Could you help me with my luggage, please?
Potrebbe darmi una mano con i bagagli, per favore?
potreb-be darmee oona mano kon ee bagal-yee pair favore

Is this a nonsmoking compartment?
È uno scompartimento non fumatori?
eh oono skomparteemento non foomatoree

Is this seat free?
È libero questo posto?
eh leebairo kwesto posto

This seat is taken
Questo posto è occupato
kwesto posto eh ok-koopato

I have reserved this seat
Questo posto è riservato
kwesto posto eh ree-sairvato

May I open/close the window?
Posso aprire/chiudere il finestrino?
pos-so apreere/k-yoodaire eel feenestreeno

When do we arrive in Bari?
A che ora arriviamo a Bari?
a ke ora arreev-yamo a baree

What station is this?
Che stazione è questa?
ke statz-yone eh kwesta

Do we stop at Pisa?
Ci fermiamo a Pisa?
chee fairmee-amo a peeza

Is there a dining car on this train?
C'è un vagone ristorante su questo treno?
cheh oon vagone reestorante soo kwesto treno

LOCAL PUBLIC TRANSPORTATION

Where is the nearest subway station?
Qual è la stazione della metropolitana più vicina?
kwal eh la statz-yone del-la metro-poleetana p-yoo veecheena

Where is the bus station?
Dov'è la stazione degli autobus/delle corriere?
doveh la statz-yone del-yee owtoboos/delle cor-riere

Which buses go to Mantua?
Quale autobus va a Mantova?
kwale owtoboos va a mantova

How often do the buses to San Gimignano run?
Ogni quanto passa l'autobus per San Gimignano?
on-yee kwanto pas-sa lowtoboos pair san jeemeen-yano

Will you let me know when we're there?
Mi potrebbe avvertire quando arriviamo là?
mee potreb-be av-verteere kwando ar-reev-yamo la

Do I have to get off yet?
Devo scendere qui?
devo shendaire kwee

How do you get to Asti?
Come posso andare ad Asti?
kome pos-so andare ad astee

I want to go to Udine
Voglio andare a Udine
vol-yo andare a oodeene

Do you go near Enna?
Passa vicino ad Enna?
pas-sa veecheeno ad en-na

Taxi and Boat

To the airport, please
All'aeroporto, per favore
alla-airoporto pair favore

How much will it cost?
Quanto mi verrà a costare?
kwanto mee vair-ra a kostare

Please stop here
Si fermi qui, per favore
see fairmee kwee pair favore

Could you wait here for me and take me back?
Può aspettarmi qui per riportarmi indietro?
pwo aspet-tarmee kwee pair reeportarmee eend-yetro

Where can I get the boat to Sirmione?
Dove posso prendere il battello per Sirmione?
dove pos-so prendaire eel bat-tello pair seerm-yone

Things You'll See

abbonamento mensile	monthly ticket
abbonamento settimanale	weekly ticket
ai binari/treni	to the platforms/trains
arrivi	arrivals
bambini	children
biglietto	ticket
biglietto d'accesso ai treni	platform ticket
biglietto giornaliero	day ticket
biglietto valido per più corse	multi-journey ticket
cambiare	to change (transportation)
cambio	exchange office
capolinea	terminal
carrozza	car (train)

→

controllo bagagli	baggage control
controllo biglietti	ticket inspection
controllo passaporti	passport control
cuccetta	sleeper car
deposito bagagli	luggage storage
diretto	long-distance train
discesa	exit
distributore automatico di biglietti	ticket machine
entrata	entrance/entry
è pericoloso sporgersi	it is dangerous to lean out
espresso	long-distance fast train
fermata	stop
Ferrovie dello Stato/FS	State Railroad
fumatori	smoking
giro in barca	boat trip
informazioni	information
la domenica	Sundays
la domenica e i giorni festivi	Sundays and holidays
libero	free
macchina obliteratrice	ticket-stamping machine
nazionale	domestic
non ferma a …	does not stop at …
non fumatori	nonsmoking
non parlare al conducente	do not speak to the driver
occupato	occupied, reserved
oggetti smarriti	lost and found
ogni abuso sarà punito con …	penalty for misuse …
ora locale	local time
orario	timetable
orario di volo	flight time
partenze	departures
passeggeri	passengers
percorso	route
porto	harbor, port
posti in piedi	standing room

→

posto (a sedere)	seat
posto prenotato	reserved seat
rapido	fast train
riservato ai non fumatori	nonsmokers only
ritardo	delay
ritiro bagagli	baggage claim
sala d'attesa	waiting room
(segnale d')allarme	emergency alarm
solo il sabato/la domenica	Saturdays/Sundays only
spuntini, panini	snacks, sandwiches
supplemento rapido	supplement for fast train
tesserino	travel card
tragitto breve	short trip
uscita	exit
uscita di sicurezza	emergency exit
vagone	car (train)
vagone letto	sleeper car
vagone ristorante	dining car
viaggio	trip
vietato fumare	no smoking
vietato l'ingresso	no entry
vietato sporgersi	do not lean out
volo	flight
volo di linea	scheduled flight

THINGS YOU'LL HEAR

Ha bagagli?
Do you have any luggage?

Fumatori o non fumatori?
Smoking or nonsmoking?

Posto vicino al corridoio o vicino al finestrino?
Window seat or aisle seat?

→

Posso vedere il vostro passaporto/biglietto, per favore?
May I see your passport/ticket, please?

Il prossimo treno parte alle diciotto
The next train leaves at 18:00

Deve cambiare a Firenze
Change at Florence

Deve pagare un supplemento
You must pay a supplement

Non ci sono più posti per Catania
There are no more seats available for Catania

I passeggeri in partenza per Roma sono pregati di recarsi all'imbarco
Passengers for Rome are requested to board

Recarsi all'uscita quattro, per favore
Please proceed to gate number four

Biglietti, prego
Tickets, please

Il treno intercity numero 687 per Roma è in partenza dal binario tre
Intercity train number 687 for Rome is leaving from platform three

Il treno regionale numero 89 da Bologna è in arrivo al binario due
Local train number 89 from Bologna is approaching platform two

Il treno espresso numero 435 da Venezia viaggia con trenta minuti di ritardo
Express train number 435 from Venice is running thirty minutes late

Apra la valigia, per favore
Open your suitcase, please

EATING OUT

There are various types of places in which to eat in Italy. For snacks, the most common is the bar. These are open all day from early morning until about 10 PM. They are all licensed to sell alcohol and usually offer a variety of sandwiches, rolls, cakes, and hot and cold drinks. In most bars you are required to first go to the cashier, place your order, pay, and get a receipt (**scontrino**). Then hand the receipt to the bartender and repeat your order. You will notice that most Italians stand up in bars—sitting down costs extra. The sign **tavola calda** means that hot dishes are also served.

For full meals there are **osteria**, **pizzeria**, **trattoria**, **taverna**, and **ristorante**. Wherever possible, it's a good idea to choose the **menu turistico** (tourist menu) or the **menu fisso** (fixed-price menu). Although the variety is more restricted, the food is of the same standard and you get a good deal more for your money, without having to face any service charge shocks at the end of the meal. Always ask for the local culinary specialties and local wine. These are generally excellent, and wine is less expensive and of superior quality in its place of origin.

In Italy, you can order the following types of coffee: **espresso** (small, strong, black coffee), **caffè macchiato** (espresso with a dash of milk), **cappuccino** (frothy, milky coffee sprinkled with cocoa), **caffelatte** (coffee with milk). These are the most common, but there is also **caffè corretto** (espresso with a liqueur), **caffè decaffeinato** (decaffeinated coffee), **caffè lungo** (weak espresso), and **caffè ristretto** (strong espresso). Remember that if you ask for "**Un caffè, per favore**," you will be served an **espresso**.

USEFUL WORDS AND PHRASES

appetizer	l'antipasto	_anteepasto_
beer	la birra	_beer-ra_
bottle	la bottiglia	_bot-teel-ya_
bread	il pane	_pane_
butter	il burro	_boor-ro_

café	il bar	*bar*
cake	la torta	*torta*
carafe	la caraffa	*karaf-fa*
check	il conto	*konto*
child's portion	una porzione per bambini	*portz-yone pair bambeenee*
coffee	il caffè	*kaf-feh*
cup	la tazza	*tatza*
dessert	il dessert	*desser*
fork	la forchetta	*forket-ta*
glass	il bicchiere	*beek-yaire*
half liter	da mezzo litro	*da metzo leetro*
knife	il coltello	*koltel-lo*
liter	un litro	*leetro*
main course	il piatto principale	*p-yat-to preencheepale*
menu	il menù	*menoo*
milk	il latte	*lat-te*
napkin	il tovagliolo	*toval-yolo*
pepper	il pepe	*pepey*
plate	il piatto	*p-yat-to*
receipt *(in bars)*	lo scontrino	*skontreeno*
(in restaurants)	la ricevuta	*reechevoota*
restaurant	il ristorante	*reestorante*
salt	il sale	*sale*
sandwich	il panino	*paneeno*
snack	lo spuntino	*spoonteeno*
soup	la minestra	*meenestra*
spoon	il cucchiaio	*kook-ya-yo*
sugar	lo zucchero	*dzookairo*
table	il tavolo	*tavolo*
tea	il tè	*teh*
teaspoon	il cucchiaino	*kook-ya-eeno*
tip	la mancia	*mancha*
waiter	il cameriere	*kamair-yaire*
waitress	la cameriera	*kamair-yaira*

water	l'acqua	_a_kwa
wine	il vino	v_ee_no
wine list	la lista dei vini	_lee_sta day v_ee_nee

A table for one/two/three, please
Un tavolo per una persona/per due/per tre, per favore
_oon t_avolo pair _oo_na pairs_o_na/pair d_oo-e_/pair tray pair fav_o_re

Is there a highchair?
Si può avere un seggiolone?
_see pwo av_ai_re oon seg-gee-olone_

May I see the menu/wine list?
Potrei vedere il menu/la lista dei vini?
_potr_ay_ ved_ai_re eel men_oo_/la l_ee_sta day v_ee_nee_

What would you recommend?
Cosa ci consiglia?
_k_o_za chee kons_ee_l-ya_

I'd like …
Vorrei …
_vor-r_ay_

Just an espresso/cappuccino/coffee with milk, please
Solo un caffè/un cappuccino/un caffelatte, per favore
_s_o_lo oon kaf-f_eh_/oon kap-pooch_ee_no/oon kaf-fel_a_t-te pair fav_o_re_

I only want a snack
Vorrei solo uno spuntino
_vor-r_ay_ s_o_lo _oo_no spoont_ee_no_

Is there a fixed-price menu?
C'è un menù fisso?
_cheh oon men_oo_ f_ee_s-so_

Can we try a local specialty/wine?
Potremmo assaggiare una specialità/un vino locale?
_potr_e_m-mo as-saj-j_a_re _oo_na spech-yal_ee_ta/oon v_ee_no lok_a_le_

A liter of house red, please
Un litro di vino rosso della casa, per favore
_oon l_eetro dee v_ee_no r_o_s-so d_e_l-la k_a_za pair fav_o_re

I'm vegetarian
Sono vegetariano
sono vejetar-y_a_no

Do you have any vegetarian dishes?
Avete piatti vegetariani?
av_e_te p-y_a_t-tee vejetar-y_a_nee

Do you have a vegetarian menu?
Avete un menu vegetariano?
av_e_te oon men_oo_ vejetar-y_a_no

Is this suitable for vegetarians?
Questo è adatto per i vegetariani?
kwesto eh ad_a_t-to pair ee vejetar-y_a_nee

I'm allergic to nuts/shellfish
Sono allergico/a alle noci/ai frutti di mare
sono al-lairjeeko/a al-lai n_o_chee/aee froot-tee dee m_a_rai

Could we have some water?
Potremmo avere un po' d'acqua?
potr_e_m-mo av_ai_re oon po d_a_kwa

Is there a children's menu?
C'è un menù per bambini?
cheh oon men_oo_ pair bamb_ee_nee

Do you do children's portions?
Fate porzioni per bambini?
f_a_tai porzeeonee pair bamb_ee_nee

Can you warm this bottle/baby food for me?
Mi può riscaldare il biberon/il pasto del bambino?
mee pwo reeskald_a_rai eel bee-bair_o_n/eel p_a_zto del bambeeno

Waiter/waitress!
Cameriere/cameriera!
kamair-y<u>ai</u>re/kamair-y<u>ai</u>ra

We didn't order this!
Non lo abbiamo ordinato!
non lo abb-y<u>a</u>mo ordeen<u>a</u>to

You've forgotten to bring my dessert
Ha dimenticato di portarmi il dessert
a deementeek<u>a</u>to dee port<u>a</u>rmee eel dess<u>e</u>r

May we have some more …?
Potremmo avere ancora un po' di …?
potr<u>e</u>m-mo av<u>ai</u>re ank<u>o</u>ra oon po dee

Can I have another knife/spoon?
Potrei avere un altro coltello/cucchiaio?
potr<u>ay</u> av<u>ai</u>re oon <u>a</u>ltro kolt<u>e</u>l-lo/kook-y<u>a</u>-yo

May we have the check please?
Può portarci il conto, per favore?
pwo port<u>a</u>rchee eel k<u>o</u>nto pair fav<u>o</u>re

Could I have a receipt, please?
Potrei avere la ricevuta/lo scontrino, per favore?
potr<u>ay</u> av<u>ai</u>re la reechev<u>oo</u>ta/lo skontr<u>ee</u>no pair fav<u>o</u>re

---

THINGS YOU'LL HEAR

Buon appetito!
Enjoy your meal!

Cosa vuole da bere?
What would you like to drink?

Avete mangiato bene?
Did you enjoy your meal?

MENU GUIDE

abbacchio alla romana	Roman-style spring lamb
acciughe sott'olio	anchovies in oil
aceto	vinegar
acqua	water
acqua minerale gassata	sparkling mineral water
acqua minerale non gassata	noncarbonated mineral water
acqua naturale	noncarbonated mineral water, tap water
affettato misto	variety of cold, sliced meats such as salami, cooked ham, etc.
affogato al caffè	ice cream with hot espresso poured over it
aglio	garlic
agnello	lamb
agnello al forno	roast lamb
albicocche	apricots
ananas	pineapple
anatra	duck
anatra all'arancia	duck in orange sauce
anguilla in umido	stewed eel
anguria	watermelon
antipasti	appetizers
antipasti misti	variety of appetizers
aperitivo	aperitif
aragosta	lobster
arancia	orange
aranciata	orangeade
aringa	herring
arista di maiale al forno	roast chine of pork
arrosto di tacchino	roast turkey
arrosto di vitello	roast veal
asparagi	asparagus
avocado all'agro	avocado pears with oil and lemon or vinegar
baccalà	dried cod
baccalà alla vicentina	Vicentine-style dried cod
bagnacauda	vegetables (usually raw) in an oil, garlic, and anchovy sauce
barbaresco	dry, red wine from the Piedmont region

barbera	dry, red wine from Piedmont
bardolino	dry red wine from area around Verona
barolo	dark, dry red wine from Piedmont
basilico	basil
bavarese	ice-cream cake with cream
bel paese	soft, high-fat white cheese
besciamella	white sauce
bignè	cream puff
birra	beer
birra chiara	light beer, lager
birra grande	large beer (approx 1 pint)
birra piccola	small beer (approx ½ pint)
birra scura	dark beer
bistecca (di manzo)	beefsteak
bistecca ai ferri	grilled steak
bollito misto con verdure	assorted boiled meats with vegetables
braciola di maiale	pork steak
branzino al forno	baked sea bass
brasato	braised beef with herbs
bresaola	dried, salted beef sliced thinly, and eaten cold with oil and lemon
brioche	type of croissant
brodo	clear broth
brodo di pollo	chicken broth
brodo vegetale	clear vegetable broth
budino	pudding
burro	butter
burro di acciughe	anchovy butter
caciotta	tender, white, medium-fat cheese from Central Italy
caffè	coffee
caffè corretto	espresso with a dash of liqueur
caffè lungo	weak espresso
caffè macchiato	espresso with a dash of milk
caffè ristretto	strong espresso
caffelatte	half coffee, half hot milk
calamari in umido	stewed squid
calamaro	squid
calzone	folded pizza with tomato and mozzarella or ricotta inside

camomilla	chamomile tea
cannella	cinnamon
cannelloni al forno	rolls of egg pasta stuffed with meat and baked in the oven
cappelle di funghi porcini alla griglia	grilled boletus mushroom caps
cappuccino	espresso coffee with foaming milk and a sprinkling of cocoa powder
capretto al forno	roast kid
carciofi	artichokes
carciofini sott'olio	baby artichokes in oil
carne	meat
carote	carrots
carpaccio	finely sliced beef fillets with oil, lemon, and grated parmesan
carré di maiale al forno	roast pork loin
cassata siciliana	Sicilian ice-cream cake with glacé fruit, chocolate, and ricotta
castagne	chestnuts
cavoletti di Bruxelles	Brussels sprouts
cavolfiore	cauliflower
cavolo	cabbage
cefalo	mullet
cernia	grouper (fish)
charlotte	ice-cream cake with milk, eggs, cream, cookies, and fruit
chianti	dark red Tuscan wine
ciambella	ring-shaped cake
cicoria	chicory
cicorino	small chicory plants
ciliege	cherries
cime di rapa	sprouting broccoli
cioccolata	chocolate
cioccolata calda	hot chocolate
cipolle	onions
cocktail di gamberetti	shrimp cocktail
conchiglie alla marchigiana	pasta shells in tomato sauce with celery, carrot, parsley, and ham
coniglio	rabbit
coniglio arrosto	roast rabbit

coniglio in umido	stewed rabbit
consommé	clear broth made with meat or chicken
contorni	vegetables
coperto	cover charge
coppa	cured neck of pork, sliced finely, and eaten cold
costata alla fiorentina	T-bone veal steak
costata di manzo	beef T-bone steak
cotechino	spiced pork sausage for boiling
cotoletta	veal, pork, or lamb chop
cotoletta ai ferri	grilled veal or pork chop
cotoletta alla milanese	veal chop in breadcrumbs
cotoletta alla valdostana	veal chop with ham and cheese cooked in breadcrumbs
cotolette di agnello	lamb chops
cotolette di maiale	pork chops
cozze	mussels
cozze alla marinara	mussels à la marinière
crema	custard dessert made with eggs and milk
crema al caffè	coffee custard dessert
crema al cioccolato	chocolate custard dessert
crema di funghi	cream of mushroom soup
crema di piselli	cream of pea soup
crema pasticciera	confectioner's custard
crêpe suzette	pancake flambéed with orange sauce
crescente	type of flat, fried Emilian bread made with flour, lard, and eggs
crespelle	type of savory pancake filled with white sauce and other fillings
crespelle ai funghi	savory pancakes with mushrooms
crespelle al formaggio	savory pancakes with cheese
crespelle al pomodoro	savory pancakes with tomato
crostata di frutta	fruit tart
dadi	bouillon cubes
datteri	dates
degustazione	tasting
degustazione di vini	wine tasting
denominazione di origine controllata (DOC)	guarantee of quality of wine
dentice al forno	baked dentex (type of sea bream)

digestivo	digestive liqueur
dolci	sweets, desserts, cakes
endivia belga	white chicory
entrecôte (di manzo)	beef entrecote
espresso	strong black coffee
fagiano	pheasant
fagioli	beans
fagioli borlotti in umido	fresh borlotti beans (type of kidney bean) cooked in vegetables, herbs, and tomato sauce
fagiolini	long, green beans
faraona	guinea fowl
fegato	liver
fegato alla veneta	liver cooked in butter with onions
fegato con salvia e burro	liver cooked in butter and sage
fettuccine	ribbon-shaped pasta
fettuccine al salmone	fettuccine with salmon
fettuccine panna e funghi	fettuccine with cream and mushrooms
fichi	figs
filetti di pesce persico	fillets of perch
filetti di sogliola	fillets of sole
filetto (di manzo)	fillet of beef
filetto ai ferri	grilled fillet of beef
filetto al cognac	fillet of beef flambé
filetto al pepe verde	fillet of beef with green peppercorns
filetto al sangue	rare fillet of beef
filetto ben cotto	well-done fillet of beef
filetto medio	medium fillet of beef
finocchio	fennel
finocchi gratinati	fennel au gratin
fonduta	cheese fondue
formaggi misti	variety of cheeses
fragole	strawberries
fragole con gelato/panna	strawberries and ice cream/cream
frappé	whisked fruit or milk drink with crushed ice
frappé al cioccolato	chocolate milk shake
frascati	dry white wine from area around Rome
frittata	type of omelette
frittata al formaggio	cheese omelette

frittata al prosciutto	ham omelette
frittata alle erbe	herb omelette
frittata alle verdure	vegetable omelette
fritto misto	mixed seafood in batter
frittura di pesce	variety of fried fish
frutta	fruit
frutta alla fiamma	fruit flambé
frutta secca	dried nuts and raisins
frutti di bosco	mixture of strawberries, raspberries, mulberries, etc.
frutti di mare	seafood
funghi	mushrooms
funghi trifolati	mushrooms fried in garlic and parsley
gamberetti	shrimp
gamberi	prawn
gamberoni	jumbo prawns
gazzosa	clear lemonade
gelatina	gelatin
gelato	ice cream
gelato con panna	ice cream with cream
gelato di crema	vanilla-flavored ice cream
gelato di frutta	fruit-flavored ice cream
gnocchetti verdi agli spinaci e al gorgonzola	small flour, potato, and spinach dumplings with melted gorgonzola
gnocchi	small flour and potato dumplings
gnocchi alla romana	small milk and semolina dumplings baked with butter
gnocchi al pomodoro	small flour and potato dumplings in tomato sauce
gorgonzola	strong, soft blue cheese from Lombardy
grancevola	spiny spider crab
granchio	crab
granita	drink with crushed ice
granita di caffè	iced coffee
granita di caffè con panna	iced coffee with cream
granita di limone	lemon drink with crushed ice
grigliata di pesce	grilled fish
grigliata mista	mixed grill (meat or fish)
grissini	thin, crisp breadsticks
gruviera	Gruyère cheese

indivia	endive
insalata	salad
insalata caprese	salad of sliced tomatoes and mozzarella
insalata di funghi porcini	boletus mushroom salad
insalata di mare	seafood salad
insalata di nervetti	boiled beef or veal served cold with beans and pickles
insalata di pomodori	tomato salad
insalata di riso	rice salad
insalata mista	mixed salad
insalata russa	Russian salad
insalata verde	green salad
involtini	meat rolls stuffed with ham and herbs
lamponi	raspberries
lamponi con gelato/panna	raspberries and ice cream/cream
lasagne al forno	layers of thick, flat pasta baked in tomato sauce, ground meat, and cheese
latte	milk
latte macchiato con cioccolato	hot, foamy milk with a sprinkling of cocoa powder
lattuga	lettuce
leggero	light
legumi	legumes
lemonsoda	sparkling lemon drink
lenticchie	lentils
lepre	hare
limonata	lemon-flavored carbonated drink
limone	lemon
lingua	tongue
lingua salmistrata	ox tongue marinaded in brine and then cooked
macedonia di frutta	fruit salad
macedonia di frutta al maraschino	fruit salad in maraschino
macedonia di frutta con gelato	fruit salad with ice cream
maiale	pork
maionese	mayonnaise
mandarino	mandarin
mandorla	almond
manzo	beef

marroni	chestnuts
marsala	very sweet wine similar to sherry
marzapane	marzipan
mascarpone	soft, sweet cheese
medaglioni di vitello	veal medallions
mela	apple
melanzane	eggplant
melanzane alla siciliana	baked eggplant slices with parmesan, tomato sauce, and egg
melone	melon
menta	mint
menu turistico	tourist menu
meringata	meringue pie
meringhe con panna	meringues with cream
merlot	dark red wine of French origin
merluzzo	cod
merluzzo alla pizzaiola	cod in tomato sauce with anchovies, capers, and parsley
merluzzo in bianco	boiled cod with oil and lemon
messicani in gelatina	rolls of veal in gelatine
millefoglie	layered pastry slice with confectioner's custard
minestra in brodo	noodle soup
minestrone	thick vegetable soup with rice or vermicelli
mirtilli	bilberries
mirtilli con gelato/panna	bilberries and ice cream/cream
more	mulberries or blackberries
more con gelato/panna	mulberries or blackberries and ice cream/cream
moscato	sweet, sparkling wine
mostarda di Cremona	preserve of glacé fruit in grape juice or sugar with syrup and mustard
mousse al cioccolato	chocolate mousse
mozzarella	firm, white, milky buffalo cheese
mozzarella in carrozza	slices of bread and mozzarella coated in flour and fried
nasello	hake
noce moscata	nutmeg
nocciole	hazelnuts

noci	walnuts
nodino	veal chop
olio	oil
orata al forno	baked gilthead (fish)
origano	oregano
ossobuco	stewed shin of veal
ostriche	oysters
paglia e fieno	mixture of plain and green tagliatelle
paillard di manzo	slices of grilled beef
paillard di vitello	slices of grilled veal
pane	bread
panino	filled roll
panna	cream
parmigiana di melanzane	baked dish of eggplant, tomato sauce, mozzarella, and parmesan
parmigiano	parmesan cheese
pasta al forno	pasta baked in white sauce and grated cheese
pasta e fagioli	very thick soup with puréed borlotti beans and small pasta rings
pasta e piselli	pasta with peas
pasticcio di fegato d'oca	baked, pasta-covered dish with goose liver
pasticcio di lepre	baked, pasta-covered dish with hare
pasticcio di maccheroni	baked macaroni
pastina in brodo	noodle soup
patate	potatoes
patate al forno	roasted potatoes
patate arrosto	roasted potatoes
patate fritte	french fries
patate in insalata	potato salad
pâté di carne	pâté
pâté di fegato	liver pâté
pâté di pesce	fish pâté
pecorino	strong, hard sheep's milk cheese
penne	pasta quills
penne ai quattro formaggi	pasta with sauce made from four cheeses
penne all'arrabbiata	pasta with tomato and chili pepper sauce
penne panna e prosciutto	pasta with cream and ham sauce
pepe	pepper (spice)

peperoni	peppers
peperoni ripieni	stuffed peppers
peperoni sott'olio	peppers in oil
pera	pear
pesca	peach
pesca melba	peach melba
pesce	fish
pesce al cartoccio	fish baked in foil with herbs
pesce in carpione	marinaded fish
pinot	dry white wine from the Veneto region
pinzimonio	assorted whole, raw vegetables eaten with oil and vinegar
piselli	peas
piselli al prosciutto	fresh peas cooked in clear broth, butter, ham, and basil
pizza Margherita	pizza with tomato and mozzarella
pizza Napoletana	pizza with tomato, mozzarella, and anchovies
pizza quattro stagioni	pizza with tomato, mozzarella, ham, mushrooms, and artichokes
pizzaiola	slices of cooked beef in tomato sauce, oregano, and anchovies
pizzoccheri alla Valtellinese	thin, pasta strips with green vegetables, melted butter, and cheese
polenta	yellow cornmeal boiled in water with salt, then left to set and cut in slices
polenta e funghi	polenta with mushrooms
polenta e latte	polenta with milk
polenta e osei	polenta with small birds
polenta pasticciata	alternate layers of polenta, tomato sauce, and cheese
pollo	chicken
pollo alla cacciatora	chicken in white wine and mushroom sauce
pollo alla diavola	chicken pieces flattened and deep-fried
pollo al forno/arrosto	roast chicken
polpette	meatballs
polpettone	meatloaf
pomodori	tomatoes
pomodori ripieni	stuffed tomatoes

pompelmo	grapefruit
porri	leeks
prezzemolo	parsley
primi piatti	first courses
prosciutto cotto	cooked ham
prosciutto crudo	type of cured ham
prosciutto di Praga	cooked ham
prosciutto e fichi	cured ham with figs
prosciutto e melone	cured ham with melon
prugne	plums
punte di asparagi all'agro	asparagus tips in oil and lemon
purè di patate	mashed potatoes
quaglie	quails
radicchio	chicory
ragù	sauce made with ground meat, tomatoes, and diced vegetables
rapa	type of white turnip with flavor similar to radish
rapanelli	radishes
ravioli	small, square-shaped egg pasta filled with meat or cheese
ravioli al pomodoro	ravioli stuffed with meat, in tomato sauce
razza	skate
ricotta	type of cottage cheese
risi e bisi	risotto with peas and small pieces of ham
riso	rice
riso al pomodoro	rice with tomato
riso in brodo	rice in clear broth
riso in insalata	rice salad
risotto	rice cooked in stock
risotto ai funghi	mushroom risotto
risotto al nero di seppia	black risotto made with cuttlefish ink
risotto al salmone	salmon risotto
risotto al tartufo	truffle risotto
risotto alla castellana	risotto with mushroom, ham, cream, and cheese sauce
risotto alla milanese	risotto flavored with saffron
roast-beef all'inglese	roast beef sliced very thinly and served cold with lemon
robiola	type of soft cheese from Lombardy

rognone trifolato	small kidney pieces in garlic, oil, and parsley
rosatello/rosato	rosé wine
rosmarino	rosemary
salame	salami
sale	salt
salmone affumicato	smoked salmon
salsa cocktail/rosa	mayonnaise and ketchup sauce for garnishing fish and seafood
salsa di pomodoro	tomato sauce
salsa tartara	tartar sauce
salsa vellutata	white sauce made with clear broth instead of milk
salsa verde	sauce for meats made with chopped parsley and oil
salsiccia	sausage
salsiccia di cinghiale	wild boar sausage
salsiccia di maiale	pork sausage
saltimbocca alla romana	slices of veal stuffed with ham and sage and fried
salvia	sage
sambuca (con la mosca)	aniseed-flavor liqueur from Lazio region served with a coffee bean in the glass
sarde ai ferri	grilled sardines
scaloppine	veal escalopes
scaloppine ai carciofi	veal escalopes with artichokes
scaloppine ai funghi	veal escalopes with mushrooms
scaloppine al Marsala	veal escalopes in Marsala
scaloppine al prezzemolo	veal escalopes with parsley
scaloppine al vino bianco	veal escalopes in white wine
scamorza alla griglia	grilled soft cheese
scampi alla griglia	grilled scampi
secco	dry
secondi piatti	second courses, main courses
sedano	celery
selvaggina	game
semifreddo	dessert made of ice cream and ladyfingers
senape	mustard
seppie in umido	stewed cuttlefish
servizio compreso	service charge included

servizio escluso	not including service charge
soave	dry white wine from region around Lake Garda
sogliola	sole
sogliola ai ferri	grilled sole
sogliola al burro	sole cooked in butter
sogliola alla mugnaia	sole cooked in flour and butter
sorbetto	sorbet, soft ice cream
soufflé al formaggio	cheese soufflé
soufflé al prosciutto	ham soufflé
spaghetti	spaghetti
spaghetti aglio, olio e peperoncino	spaghetti with garlic, oil, and crushed chili pepper
spaghetti al pesto	spaghetti in crushed basil, garlic, oil, and parmesan dressing
spaghetti al pomodoro	spaghetti in tomato sauce
spaghetti al ragù	spaghetti with meat sauce
spaghetti alla carbonara	spaghetti with egg, chopped bacon, and cheese sauce
spaghetti alla puttanesca	spaghetti with anchovies, capers, and black olives in tomato sauce
spaghetti alle vongole	spaghetti with clams
spaghetti all'amatriciana	spaghetti with chopped bacon and tomato sauce, typical of Rome
speck	type of cured, smoked ham
spezzatino di vitello	veal stew
spiedini	small pieces of assorted meats or fish cooked on a spit
spinaci	spinach
spinaci all'agro	spinach with oil and lemon
spremuta d'arancia	freshly squeezed orange juice
spremuta di limone	freshly squeezed lemon juice
spumante	sparkling wine
stracchino	type of soft cheese from Lombardy
stracciatella	soup of beaten eggs cooked in boiling, clear broth
strudel di mele	apple strudel
succo d'arancia	orange juice
succo di albicocca	apricot juice
succo di pera	pear juice

succo di pesca	peach juice
succo di pompelmo	grapefruit juice
sugo al tonno	tomato sauce with garlic, tuna, and parsley
tacchino ripieno	stuffed turkey
tagliata	finely cut beef fillet cooked in the oven
tagliatelle	thin, flat strips of egg pasta
tagliatelle al basilico	tagliatelle and chopped basil
tagliatelle alla bolognese	tagliatelle with ground meat and tomato sauce
tagliatelle al pomodoro	tagliatelle with tomato sauce
tagliatelle al ragù	tagliatelle with ground meat and tomato sauce
tagliatelle con panna e funghi	tagliatelle with cream and mushroom sauce
tagliatelle rosse	tagliatelle with chopped red peppers
tagliatelle verdi	tagliatelle with chopped spinach
tagliolini	thin soup noodles
tagliolini ai funghi	tagliolini with mushrooms
tagliolini alla panna	tagliolini with cream
tagliolini al salmone	tagliolini with salmon
tartine	small sandwiches
tartufo	round ice cream covered in cocoa or chocolate
tè	tea
tè con latte	tea with milk
tè con limone	lemon tea
tiramisù	dessert made with coffee-soaked ladyfingers, eggs, Marsala, mascarpone, and cocoa powder
tonno	tuna
torta	tart, flan
torta salata	savory flan
torta ai carciofi	artichoke flan
torta al cioccolato	chocolate tart
torta al formaggio	cheese flan
torta di mele	apple tart
torta di noci	walnut tart
torta di ricotta	type of cheesecake
torta di zucchine	zucchini flan
torta gelato	ice-cream tart

tortellini	small pasta shapes filled with ground pork, ham, parmesan, and nutmeg
tortellini alla panna	tortellini with cream
tortellini al pomodoro	tortellini with tomato sauce
tortellini al ragù	tortellini with ground meat and tomato sauce
tortellini in brodo	tortellini in clear broth
tortelloni di magro/di ricotta	pasta shapes filled with cheese, parsley, chopped vegetables
tortelloni di zucca	tortelloni stuffed with pumpkin
trancio di palombo	smooth dogfish steak
trancio di pesce spada	swordfish steak
trenette col pesto	type of flat spaghetti with crushed basil, garlic, oil, and cheese sauce
triglie	mullet (fish)
trippa	tripe
trota	trout
trota affumicata	smoked trout
trota al burro	trout cooked in butter
trota alle mandorle	trout with almonds
trota bollita	boiled trout
uccelletti	small birds wrapped in bacon, served on cocktail sticks
uova	eggs
uova al tegamino con pancetta	fried eggs and bacon
uova alla coque	boiled eggs
uova farcite	eggs with tuna, capers, and mayonnaise filling
uova sode	hard-boiled eggs
uva	grapes
uva bianca	white grapes
uva nera	black grapes
vellutata di asparagi	creamed asparagus with egg yolks
vellutata di piselli	creamed peas with egg yolks
verdura	vegetables
vermicelli	very fine, thin pasta, often used in soups
vino	wine
vino bianco	white wine
vino da dessert	dessert wine
vino da pasto	table wine

vino da tavola	table wine
vino rosso	red wine
vitello	veal
vitello tonnato	cold sliced veal in tuna, anchovy, oil, and lemon sauce
vongole	clams
würstel	hot dog
zabaione	creamy dessert made from beaten eggs, sugar, and Marsala
zafferano	saffron
zucca	pumpkin
zucchine	zucchini
zucchine al pomodoro	chopped zucchini in tomato, garlic, and parsley sauce
zucchine ripiene	stuffed zucchini
zuccotto	ice-cream cake with ladyfingers, cream, and chocolate
zuppa	soup
zuppa di cipolle	onion soup
zuppa di cozze	mussel soup
zuppa di lenticchie	lentil soup
zuppa di pesce	fish soup
zuppa di verdura	vegetable soup
zuppa inglese	trifle

STORES AND SERVICES

This chapter covers all kinds of shopping needs and services. To start with you'll find some general phrases that can be used in lots of different places—many of these are listed below. After the general phrases come more specific requests and sentences to use when you've found what you need, be it food, clothing, repairs, film-developing, a haircut, or bargaining in the market. Don't forget to refer to the mini-dictionary for items you may be looking for.

Stores are usually open from 8:30 or 9 AM to 12:30 or 1 PM and from 3:30 or 4 PM to 7:30 or 8 PM, and often later in tourist resorts in peak season. Store hours may vary slightly according to the region you are in, and stores may close on different days of the week—often on Monday mornings, all day Monday, or on Thursday afternoons. Venice has half-day closing (only in winter) on Monday mornings. In Florence, stores are closed on Monday mornings or all day Monday in the winter, fall, and spring, and are closed on Saturday afternoons in August. Most large stores and supermarkets are open Monday to Saturday.

It's acceptable to bargain in the market, but only if the price is not displayed.

In Italy, **chili** (kilos) and **etti** (hectograms) are used. One **etto** = 100 grams. Cheese, ham, etc., are generally sold by the **etto** and fruit and vegetables by the **chili**.

Pharmacies are very expensive in Italy (see Health, page 113). If you should need items such as antiseptic cream, toothpaste, bandages, tampons, etc., it's better to go to a supermarket or a **drogheria** (*drogairee-a*), which is like a drugstore and general grocery store combined. If you wish to buy perfume or sophisticated cosmetic products, you should go to a **profumeria** (*profoomairee-a*). If you want to buy film or get your photos developed, go to a photographic store or an optician's, not to a pharmacy.

In Italy, you won't find the type of Laundromat where you can do your own washing and drying. A dry cleaner's will only accept clothes for dry cleaning or large items such as bed linen, but not small personal items.

For cigarettes, stamps, chewing gum, and postcards, go to a **tabaccaio,** which can be identified by a sign with a white **T** on a black background. A **tabaccaio** generally has the same opening hours as stores. After 8 PM, you can only buy cigarettes in specially licensed bars or in train stations.

Useful Words and Phrases

antiques shop	il negozio di antiquariato	*negotz-yo dee anteekwar-yato*
audio equipment store	il negozio di hi-fi	*negotz-yo dee 'hi-fi'*
bakery	la panetteria	*panet-tairee-a*
bookstore	la libreria	*leebrairee-a*
butcher shop	la macelleria	*machel-lairee-a*
buy	comprare	*komprare*
camera store	il negozio di macchine fotografiche	*negotz-yo dee mak-keene fotografeeke*
camping equipment	l'attrezzatura da campeggio	*at-tretz-zatoora da kampej-jo*
candy store	la pasticceria	*pasteech-chairee-a*
cash register	la cassa	*kas-sa*
china	la porcellana	*porchel-lana*
cost	prezzo	*pretzo*
craft store	il negozio di artigianato	*negotz-yo dee arteejanato*
department store	il grande magazzino	*grande magatzeeno*
(large)	l'ipermecato	*eepairmairkato*
dry cleaner's	la lavanderia a secco, la tintoria	*lavandairee-a a sek-ko, teentoree-a*

electrical goods store	il negozio di articoli elettrici	*negotz-yo dee arteekolee elet-treechee*
expensive	caro, costoso	*karo, kostozo*
fish market	la pescheria	*peskairee-a*
florist's	fioraio	*f-yora-yo*
fruit	la frutta	*froot-ta*
gift shop	il negozio di articoli da regalo	*negotz-yo dee arteekolee da regalo*
grocery store	l'alimentari	*aleementaree*
hair salon (*men's*)	barbiere	*barb-yaire*
(*women's*)	parrucchiere, acconciature	*par-rookk-yaire, ak-konchatoore*
hardware store	il ferramenta	*fair-ramenta*
indoor market	il mercato coperto	*mairkato kopairto*
inexpensive	economico	*ekonomeeko*
jeweler's	la gioielleria	*joyel-lairee-a*
market	il mercato	*mairkato*
menswear	l'abbigliamento da uomo	*ab-beel-yamento da womo*
newsstand	l'edicola	*edeecola*
optician's	il ottico	*ot-teeko*
pastry shop	la pasticceria	*pasteechairee-a*
pharmacy	la farmacia	*farmachee-a*
produce market	il negozio di frutta e verdura	*negotz-yo dee froot-ta ay verdoora*
receipt	lo scontrino	*skontreeno*
record store	il negozio di dischi	*negotz-yo dee deeskee*
sale	la svendita, i saldi	*zvendeeta, saldee*
shoe repairer's	il calzolaio	*kaltzola-yo*
shoe store	il negozio di scarpe	*negotz-yo dee skarpe*
shopping bag	il sacchetto	*sak-ket-to*
souvenir store	il negozio di souvenir	*negotz-yo dee sooveneer*
sports equipment	l'attrezzatura sportiva	*at-tretz-zatoora sporteeva*

81

sportswear	l'abbigliamento sportivo	*ab-beel-yamento sporteevo*
stationery store	la cartoleria	*kartolairee-a*
store	il negozio	*negotz-yo*
supermarket	il supermercato	*soopairmairkato*
tailor	il sarto	*sarto*
tobacco shop	il tabaccaio	*tabak-ka-yo*
toy store	il negozio di giocattoli	*negotz-yo dee jokat-tolee*
travel agent	l'agenzia di viaggio	*ajentzee-a dee vee-aj-jo*
vegetables	la verdura	*vairdoora*
wine merchant	la enoteca	*enotaika*
women's wear	l'abbigliamento per signora	*ab-beel-yamento pair seen-yora*

Excuse me, where is/where are …?
Mi scusi, dov'è/dove sono …?
mee skoozee doveh/dove sono

Where is there a … (store)?
Dov'è un negozio di … qui vicino?
doveh oon negotz-yo dee … kwee veecheeno

Where is the … department?
Dov'è il reparto …?
doveh eel reparto

Where is the main shopping area?
Dov'è la zona dei negozi?
doveh la zona day negotzi

Is there a market here?
C'è un mercato qui?
cheh oon mairkato kwee

I'd like …
Vorrei …
vor-ray

Do you have …?
Avete …?
avete

How much is this?
Quanto costa questo?
kwanto kosta kwesto

Where do I pay?
Dove si paga?
dove see paga

Do you take credit cards?
Accettate carte di credito?
ach-chet-tate karte dee kredeeto

I think perhaps you've shortchanged me
Penso che abbiate sbagliato nel darmi il resto
penso ke abb-yate sbal-yato nel darmee eel resto

Can I have a receipt/a bag, please?
Potrebbe darmi lo scontrino/un sacchetto?
potreb-be darmee lo skontreeno/oon sak-ket-to

I'm just looking
Sto solo dando un'occhiata
sto solo dando oon okk-yata

I'll come back later
Tornerò più tardi
tornairo p-yoo tardee

Do you have any more of these?
Ne ha ancora di questi?
ne a ankora dee kwestee

Do you have anything less expensive?
Non ha niente di più economico?
non a n-yente dee p-yoo ekonomeeko

Do you have anything larger/smaller?
Non ne ha uno più grande/piccolo?
non ne a oono p-yoo grande/peek-kolo

Can I try it/them on?
Posso provarlo/provarli?
pos-so provarlo/provarlee

Does it come in other colors?
C'è anche in altri colori?
cheh anke een altree koloree

Could you gift wrap it for me?
Può farmi un pacchetto regalo?
pwo farmee oon pak-ket-to regalo

I'd like to exchange this; it's defective
Vorrei cambiare questo: è difettoso
vor-ray kamb-yare kwesto: eh deefet-tozo

I'm afraid I don't have the receipt
Mi dispiace, ma non ho lo scontrino
mee deesp-yache ma non o lo skontreeno

Can I have a refund?
Posso riavere indietro i soldi?
pos-so ree-avaire endee-etro ee soldee

My camera isn't working
La mia macchina fotografica non funziona
la mee-a mak-keena fotografeeka non foontz-yona

I want a roll of 36-exposure color film, 100 ISO
Vorrei una pellicola 100ISO a colori da 36 foto
vor-ray oona pel-leekola 100 ee-esse-o a koloree da 36 foto

I'd like this film processed
Vorrei sviluppare questa pellicola
vor-ray sveeloop-pare kwesta pel-leekola

Matte/glossy prints
Fotografie su carta opaca/lucida
fotografee-e soo karta opaka/loocheeda

One-hour service, please
Vorrei il servizio in un'ora, per favore
vor-ray eel serveetz-yo een oon ora pair favore

Where can I get this repaired?
Dove posso farlo riparare?
dove pos-so farlo reeparare

Can you repair this?
Può aggiustarmelo?
pwo aj-joostarmelo

I'd like this skirt/these pants dry-cleaned
Vorrei far lavare a secco questa gonna/questi pantaloni
vor-ray far lavarai a sec-co kwesta gon-na/kwestee pantalonee

When will it/they be ready?
Quando sarà pronto/saranno pronti?
kwando sara pronto/saran-no prontee

I'd like to make an appointment
Vorrei prendere un appuntamento
vor-ray prendaire oon ap-poontamento

I want a cut and blow-dry
Vorrei taglio e messa in piega (con il föhn)
vor-ray tal-yo ay mes-sa een p-yega kon eel fon

With conditioner/No conditioner, thanks
Con il balsamo/Senza il balsamo, grazie
kon eel bal-samo/sentza eel bal-samo gratzee-e

Just a trim, please
Solo una spuntatina, per favore
solo oona spoontateena pair favore

Not too much off!
Non tagli troppo!
non tal-yee trop-po

When does the market open?
Quando apre il mercato?
kwando apre eel mairkato

What's the price per kilo?
Quanto costa al chilo?
kwanto kosta al keelo

Could you write that down?
Può scriverlo?
pwo skreevairlo

That's too much! I'll pay …
È troppo! Le do …
eh trop-po! le do

Could I have a discount?
Potrebbe farmi uno sconto?
potreb-be farmee oono skonto

That's fine. I'll take it!
Va bene. Lo prendo!
va bene. lo prendo

I'll have a piece of that cheese
Vorrei un pezzo di quel formaggio
vor-ray oon petz-zo dee kwel formaj-jo

About 250/500 grams
Circa duecentocinquanta/cinquecento grammi
cheerka doo-e-chentocheenkwanta/cheenkwechento gram-mee

A kilo/half a kilo of apples, please
Un chilo/mezzo chilo di mele, per favore
oon keelo/metzo keelo dee mele pair favore

250 grams of that cheese, please
Due etti e mezzo di quel formaggio, per favore
doo-e et-tee ay metzo dee kwel formaj-jo pair favore

May I taste it?
Posso assaggiarlo?
pos-so as-saj-jarlo

That's very nice, I'll take some
Quello è molto buono; ne prenderò un po'
kwel-lo eh molto bwono; ne prendairo oon po

It isn't what I wanted
Non è quello che volevo
non eh kwel-lo ke volevo

THINGS YOU'LL SEE

abbigliamento da uomo	men's clothing
abbigliamento per signora	women's clothing
acconciature	women's hair salon
agenzia di viaggio	travel agency
alimentari	grocery store
barbiere	barber's
calzature	shoes
cartoleria	stationery store
cassa	cashier, cash register
coiffeur	hairstylist
colpi di sole	highlights
dolci	confectionery, cakes
dozzina	dozen
elettrodomestici	electrical appliances
entrata	entrance

→

fai-da-te	hardware store
fioraio	florist
forniture per ufficio	office supplies
fresco	fresh
giocattoli	toys
grande magazzino	department store
la merce venduta non si cambia senza lo scontrino	goods are not exchanged without a receipt
libreria	bookstore
liquori	liquor
macelleria	butcher shop
messa in piega con il föhn	blow-dry
moda	fashion
munitevi di un carrello/cestino	please take a cart/basket
pagare alla cassa	pay at the desk
panetteria	bakery
parrucchiere (per signora)	women's hair salon
pasticceria	pastry store
pellicceria	furrier
permanente	perm
pescheria	fish market
piano superiore	upper floor
prezzo	price
prima qualità	high quality
reparto	department
ridotto	reduced
riviste	magazines
saldi	sales
sartoria	tailor's
spingere	push
spuntata	trim
svendita	sale
tabacchi	tobacco
taglio	cut

→

tirare	pull
uscita	exit
verdure	vegetables

THINGS YOU'LL HEAR

Desidera?
Can I help you?

La stanno servendo?
Are you being served?

Non ha spiccioli?
Do you have anything smaller? (money)

Mi dispiace quest'articolo è esaurito
I'm sorry, we're out of stock

Questo è tutto quello che abbiamo
This is all we have

Ha spiccioli/moneta?
Do you have any change?

Diamo solamente buoni acquisto
We only give gift vouchers

Si accomodi alla cassa, prego
Please pay at the register

Nient'altro?
Will there be anything else?

Quanto ne vuole?
How much would you like?

Come lo desidera?
How would you like it?

SPORTS

Whether you enjoy sports as a passive spectator or as an active participant, Italy has a great deal to offer. The Italians are passionate soccer fans, and the championships are played from September to May, with international matches throughout the year. Bicycling is also a favorite Italian sport, and the **Giro d'Italia**—the annual race around the peninsula—takes place during May and June.

Summer sports include fishing, golf, skin diving, swimming, and tennis. There is no lack of fine beaches in Italy, and most of them are well-managed and provide everything for the tourist's enjoyment. There are numerous windsurfing schools where you can take lessons and rent all the necessary equipment, from boards to wet suits. One of the most notable areas for this sport is Lake Garda.

Italy is a haven for mountain climbers and hikers, who will delight in discovering the many beautiful Alpine and Apennine valleys unknown to the average tourist. For winter sports there are excellently equipped skiing resorts in the Dolomites and in the Piedmont and Lombardy regions of Northern Italy.

USEFUL WORDS AND PHRASES

athletics	l'atletica	atl*e*teeka
ball	la palla	p*a*l-la
beginners' slope	la pista per principianti	p*ee*sta pair preencheep-y*a*ntee
bicycle	la bicicletta	beecheeckl*e*t-ta
bicycling	il ciclismo	cheekl*ee*zmo
go bicycling	andare in bicicletta	and*a*re een beecheeckl*e*t-ta
binding (*ski*)	l'attacco (degli sci)	at-t*a*k-ko d*e*l-yee shee
cable car	la funivia	fooneev*ee*-a
canoe/canoeing	la canoa	kan*o*-a
chairlift	la seggiovia	sej-jov*ee*-a

cross-country skiing	lo sci di fondo	*shee dee fondo*
dive	tuffarsi	*toof-farsee*
diving board	il trampolino	*trampoleeno*
downhill skiing	lo sci da discesa	*shee da deesheza*
fishing	la pesca	*peska*
fishing rod	la canna da pesca	*kan-na da peska*
flippers	le pinne	*peen-ne*
game (*match*)	la partita	*parteeta*
goggles	gli occhialetti	*ok-kyalet-ti*
golf course	il campo da golf	*kampo da 'golf'*
play golf	giocare a golf	*jokare a 'golf'*
gymnastics	la ginnastica	*jeen-nasteeka*
hang gliding	il deltaplano	*deltaplano*
harpoon	l'arpione	*arp-yone*
hunting	la caccia	*kach-cha*
ice hockey	l'hockey su ghiaccio	*'hockey' soo g-yach-cho*
mask	la maschera	*maskaira*
mast	l'albero	*albairo*
mountaineering	l'alpinismo	*alpeeneezmo*
oxygen bottles	le bombole di ossingeno	*bombolay dee os-seejeno*
parasailing	il parapendio	*parapendee-o*
pedal boat	il pedalò	*pedalo*
race track	la pista	*peesta*
racket	la racchetta	*rak-ket-ta*
ride	andare a cavallo	*andare a kaval-lo*
riding	l'equitazione	*ekweetatz-yone*
riding hat	il cappello da fantino	*kap-pel-lo da fanteeno*
rock climbing	l'alpinismo	*alpeeneezmo*
saddle	la sella	*sel-la*
sail	la vela	*vela*
sailboard	il surf	*'surf'*
sailing	andare a vela	*andare a vela*
shooting range	il tiro a segno	*teero a sen-yo*
skate	pattinare	*pat-teenare*
skates	i pattini	*pat-teenee*

skating rink	la pista di pattinaggio	_peesta dee pateenaj-jo_
ski (*verb*)	sciare	_shee-are_
ski boots	gli scarponi da sci	_skarponee da shee_
skiing	lo sci	_shee_
skin diving	l'immersione subacquea	_eem-mairsyone soobakwe-a_
ski pass	lo ski pass	_'ski pass'_
ski poles	i bastoncini	_bastoncheenee_
skis	gli sci	_shee_
ski tow	lo skilift	_'skilift'_
ski trail	la pista da sci	_peesta da shee_
ski wax	la sciolina	_shee-oleena_
sled	la slitta	_zleeta_
snorkel	boccaglio	_bok-kalyo_
soccer	il calcio	_kalcho_
soccer ball	il pallone	_pal-lone_
soccer match	la partita di calcio	_parteeta dee kalcho_
sports center	il centro sportivo	_chentro sporteevo_
stadium	lo stadio	_stad-yo_
surfboard	il surf	_'surf'_
swim	nuotare	_nwotare_
swimming pool	la piscina	_peesheena_
team	la squadra	_skwadra_
tennis court	il campo da tennis	_kampo da ten-nis_
toboggan	la slitta	_zleeta_
underwater fishing	la pesca subacquea	_peska soobakwe-a_
volleyball	pallavolo	_pal-lavolo_
water-ski	fare sci d'acqua	_fare shee dakwa_
water-skiing	lo sci d'acqua	_shee dakwa_
water skis	gli sci d'acqua	_shee dakwa_
wet suit	la muta da sub	_moota da soob_
go windsurfing	praticare il windsurf	_prateekare eel 'windsurf'_

How do I get to the beach?
Potrebbe indicarmi la strada per la spiaggia?
potreb-be eendeekarmee la strada pair la sp-yaj-ja

How deep is the water here?
Quant'è profonda qui l'acqua?
kwanteh profonda kwee lakwa

Is there an indoor/outdoor pool here?
C'è una piscina coperta/scoperta?
cheh oona peesheena kopairta/skopairta

Is it dangerous to swim here?
È pericoloso nuotare qui?
eh paireekolozo nwotare kwee

Can I fish here?
Posso pescare qui?
pos-so peskare kwee

Do I need a license?
C'è bisogno della licenza?
cheh beezon-yo del-la leechentza

Is there a golf course near here?
C'è un campo da golf da queste parti?
cheh oon kampo da 'golf' da kweste partee

Do I have to be a member?
È necessario essere socio?
eh neches-sar-yo es-saire socho

Where can I rent ...?
Dove posso noleggiare ...?
dove pos-so nolej-jare

I would like to rent a bike/some skis
Vorrei noleggiare una bicicletta/degli sci
vor-ray nolej-jare oona beecheeklet-ta/del-yee shee

How much does it cost per hour/day?
Quanto costa all'ora/al giorno?
kwanto kosta al ora/al jorno

When does the lift start?
A che ora aprono gli impianti?
a ke ora aprono l-yee eemp-yantee

What are the snow conditions like today?
Quali sono le condizioni della neve oggi?
kwalee sono le kondeetz-yonee del-la neve oj-jee

How much is a daily/weekly lift pass?
Quanto costa un abbonamento giornaliero/settimanale?
kwanto kosta oon ab-bonamento jornal-yairo/set-tee-manale

I would like to take skiing lessons
Vorrei prendere lezioni di sci
vor-ray prendaire letz-yonee dee shee

Where are the beginners' slopes?
Dove sono le discese per principianti?
dove sono le deesheze pair preencheep-yantee

Is it very steep?
È molto ripido?
eh molto reepeedo

I would like to take water-skiing lessons
Vorrei prendere lezioni di sci d'acqua
vor-ray prendaire letz-yonee dee shee dakwa

There's something wrong with this binding
C'è qualcosa che non va in questo attacco
cheh kwalkoza ke non va een kwesto at-tak-ko

I haven't played this before
Non ho mai provato prima
non o mi provato preema

Let's go skating/swimming
Andiamo a pattinare/sciare
and-yamo a pat-teenare/shee-are

What's the score?
A quanto sono?
a kwanto sono

Who won?
Chi ha vinto?
kee a veento

THINGS YOU'LL SEE

alla seggiovia	to the chairlift
correnti pericolose	dangerous currents
divieto di balneazione	no bathing
divieto di pesca	no fishing
funivia	cable car
noleggio barche	boat rental
noleggio biciclette	bicycle rental
noleggio sci	ski rental
non dondolarsi	no swinging
pedoni	pedestrians
pericolo	danger
pericolo di valanghe	danger of avalanches
piscina coperta	indoor swimming pool
piscina scoperta	outdoor swimming pool
pista ciclabile	bicycle path
pista da fondo	cross-country ski track
pista facile/difficile	easy/difficult slope
pista per slitte	toboggan run
prepararsi a scendere	get ready to alight
pronto soccorso	first aid
sci di fondo	cross-country skiing
scuola di sci	ski school
trampolino	diving board; ski jump
vietato bagnarsi	no bathing
vietato pescare	no fishing
vietato tuffarsi	no diving

POST OFFICES AND BANKS

Main post offices are open from 8:15 AM to 7 PM, while local offices generally close at 2 PM. Mailboxes in Italy are generally red, although there are some yellow ones. Stamps can be bought at the post office or, more conveniently, at any **tabaccaio** (tobacco shop). These are easily identified by the sign displayed outside—a white **T** on a black background.

Banks are open from 8:30 AM to 1:30 PM and from 2:45 PM to 3:45 PM, from Monday to Friday. Generally speaking, it is better to change money in a bank than in an exchange office (called **cambio** or **cambiavalute**), because the latter charges a commission. Exchange offices are found in airports, in train stations, and in the city center. In larger cities, you will find automatic exchange offices with ATMs outside some banks.

You will find ATMs for bank and credit cards outside the main banks (but a commission of about five percent is charged if you draw money with a credit card). Major credit cards are generally accepted in hotels, restaurants, and stores. Small stores or restaurants do not accept them.

The Italian unit of currency is the common European currency, the **euro** (*ayoo-ro*). One **euro** is divided into 100 **centesimi** (*chen-teseemee*), and the coins come in 1, 2, 5, 10, 20, and 50 **centesimi**; 1 and 2 **euros**. Bills are available in 5, 10, 20, 50, 100, 200, and 500 **euros**.

USEFUL WORDS AND PHRASES

airmail	la posta aerea	*posta a-aire-a*
ATM	lo sportello automatico	*sportel-lo owtomateeko*
bank	la banca	*banka*
bill (*money*)	la banconota	*bankonota*
cash (*noun*)	il denaro	*denaro*
change (*verb*)	cambiare	*kamb-yare*
check	l'assegno	*as-sen-yo*

checkbook	il libretto degli assegni	*leebret-to del-yee as-sen-yee*
collection	la levata	*levata*
counter	lo sportello	*sportel-lo*
credit card	la carta di credito	*karta dee kredeeto*
customs form	il modulo per la dogana	*modoolo pair la dogana*
delivery	la consegna	*konsen-ya*
deposit *(noun)*	il deposito	*depozeeto*
(verb)	depositare	*depozeetare*
envelope	la busta	*boosta*
exchange rate	il tasso di cambio	*tas-so dee kam-bee-o*
fax *(noun)*	il fax	*'fax'*
(verb)	spedire via fax	*spedeere vee-a 'fax'*
fax machine	il fax	*'fax'*
form	il modulo	*modoolo*
general delivery	fermo posta	*fairmo posta*
international money order	il vaglia postale internazionale	*val-ja postale eentairnatz-yonale*
letter	la lettera	*let-taira*
letter carrier	il postino	*posteeno*
mail *(noun)*	la posta	*posta*
(verb)	spedire	*spedeere*
mailbox	la cassetta delle lettere	*cas-set-ta del-le let-taire*
money order	il vaglia postale	*val-ya postale*
package/parcel	il pacchetto, il pacco	*pak-ket-to, pak-ko*
postage rates	le tariffe postali	*tareef-fe postalee*
postal order	il vaglia postale	*val-ya postale*
postcard	la cartolina	*kartoleena*
post office	l'ufficio postale	*oof-feecho postale*
registered letter	la raccomandata	*rak-komandata*
stamp	il francobollo	*frankobol-lo*
surface mail	la posta ordinaria	*posta ordeengree-a*
telegram	il telegramma	*telegram-ma*

traveler's check	il traveller's cheque	*'traveler's check'*
withdraw	prelevare	*prelevare*
zip code	il codice di avvia- mento postale	*kodeeche dee avv- yamento postale*

How much is a postcard to …?
Quanto costa spedire una cartolina in …?
kwanto kosta spedeere oona kartoleena een

I would like three 60-cent stamps
Vorrei tre francobolli da settanta centesimi
vor-ray tre frankobol-lee da set-tanta chen-teseemee

I want to register this letter
Vorrei spedire questa lettera per raccomandata
vor-ray spedeere kwesta let-taira pair rak-komandata

I want to send this package to …
Vorrei spedire questo pacco in …
vor-ray spedeere kwesto pak-ko een

How long does the mail to … take?
Quanto ci mette la posta per arrivare in …?
kwanto chee met-te la posta pair ar-reevare een

Where can I mail this?
Dove posso imbucarlo?
dove pos-so eembookarlo

Is there any mail for me?
C'è posta per me?
cheh posta pair me

I'd like to send a fax
Vorrei spedire un fax
vor-ray spedeere oon fax

This is to go airmail
Deve essere spedito per via aerea
deve es-saire spedeeto pair vee-a a-aire-a

I'd like to change this into 10 euro bills
Vorrei cambiare in banconote da dieci euro
vor-ray kamb-yare een bankonote da dee-echee ayoo-ro

Can I cash these traveler's checks?
Posso cambiare questi traveller's cheques?
pos-so kamb-yare kwestee 'traveler's checks'

What is the exchange rate for the dollar?
Qual è il tasso di cambio della dolar?
kwaleh eel tas-so dee kam-bee-o del-la dahlar

Can I draw cash using this credit card?
Posso fare un prelievo usando la carta di credito?
pos-so fare oon prel-yevo oozando la karta dee kredeeto

I'd like it in 20 euro bills
Vorrei banconote da venti euro
vor-ray bankonote da ventee ayoo-ro

Could you give me smaller bills?
Può darmi banconote di piccolo taglio?
pwo darmee bankonote dee peek-kolo tal-yo

THINGS YOU'LL SEE

affrancatura	postage
affrancatura per l'estero	postage abroad
assicurata	insured mail
cambiavalute/cambio	currency exchange office
cartolina	postcard
codice (di avviamento) postale	zip code
compilare	to fill in
conto corrente	current account
deposito	deposit
destinatario	addressee

→

espresso	express
fermo posta	general delivery
francobollo	stamp
indirizzo	address
lettera	letter
orario di apertura	opening hours
mittente	sender
pacchetto	package
posta	mail
posta aerea	airmail
prelievo	withdrawal
raccomandata	registered letter
riempire	to fill in
sportello	counter
sportello pacchi	packages counter
tariffa	rate, charge
tariffa interna	domestic postage

COMMUNICATIONS

Telephones: Old telephone boxes can be operated with **gettoni** – tokens – but they are being replaced with newer phones which take phonecards. These cost 1, 2.5, 5, or 8 euros and can be bought at newsstands. You need to snap off the corner of the card to start using it.

If you want to make a long-distance phone call, it is better to go to an office of the Italian national telephone company, the **Telecom Italia**, which is a department of the main post office in Florence and Venice. Or, you can ask in a bar if the bartender has **un telefono a scatti**—you make your call first and are then charged for the number of units you have used. To call the US, dial 001 followed by the area code and the subscriber's number.

The tones you'll hear when telephoning in Italy are:

Dial tone: two tones, one short and one long, at regular intervals;
Ringing tone: one single, long tone at regular intervals;
Busy signal: short rapid beeps.

USEFUL WORDS AND PHRASES

answering machine	la segretaria telefonica	*segretaree_a telef_oneeka*
call *(noun)*	la telefonata	*telefon_ata*
(verb)	telefonare	*telefon_are*
cardphone	il telefono a scheda	*tel_efono a sk_eda*
code	il prefisso	*pref_ees-so*
collect call	la chiamata a carico del destinatario	*k-yam_ata a k_areeko del desteenat_aree-o*
crossed wires	l'interferenza	*eentairfair_entza*
dial	fare il numero	*f_are eel n_oomairo*
dial tone	il segnale di libero	*sen-y_ale dee l_eebairo*

101

directory assistance	il servizio informazioni telefoniche	*sairveetz-yo eenformatz-yonee telefoneeke*
email	la posta elettronica	*posta ai-lait-tronee-ka*
emergency	l'emergenza	*emairjentza*
extension	l'interno	*eentairno*
fax machine	il fax	*'fax'*
international call	la chiamata internazionale	*k-yamata eentairnatz-yonale*
internet	l'internet	*'internet'*
mobile phone	il telefonino	*telefonino*
modem	il modem	*'modem'*
number	il numero	*noomairo*
operator	l'operatore	*opairatore*
payphone	il telefono a gettoni	*telefono a jet-tonee*
phonecard	la scheda telefonica	*skeda telefoneeka*
photocopier	la fotocopiatrice	*fotokopee-atreece*
receiver	il ricevitore	*reecheveetore*
telephone	il telefono	*telefono*
telephone booth	la cabina telefonica	*kabeena telefoneeka*
website	il sito internet	*seeto 'internet'*
wrong number	il numero sbagliato	*noomairo zbal-yato*

Where is the nearest telephone booth?
Dov'è la cabina telefonica più vicina?
doveh la kabeena telefoneeka p-yoo veecheena

Is there a phone book?
C'è una guida telefonica?
cheh oona gweeda telefoneeka

Can I call abroad from here?
Posso fare una telefonata internazionale da qua?
pos-so fare oona telefonata eentairnatz-yonale da kwa

I would like to make a collect call
La metta a carico del destinatario
la met-ta a kareeko del desteenataree-o

I would like a number in …
Ho bisogno del numero di un abbonato di …
o beezon-yo del noomairo dee oon ab-bonato dee

How do I get an outside line?
Come devo fare per avere una linea esterna?
kome devo fare pair avaire oona leene-a estairna

Hello, this is … speaking
Pronto, sono …
pronto sono

Is that …?
Parlo con …?
parlo kon

Speaking
Sono io/pronto
sono ee-o/pronto

I would like to speak to …
Vorrei parlare con …
vor-ray parlare kon

Extension …, please
Interno …, per favore
eentairno … pair favore

Please tell him/her … called
Per cortesia, gli/le dica che ha telefonato …
pair kortezee-a l-yee/le deeka ke a telefonato

Ask him/her to call me back, please
Mi fa richiamare, per favore
mee fa reekeeamare, pair favore

My number is …
Il mio numero è …
eel mee-o noomairo eh

Do you know where he/she is?
Non sa dov'è?
non sa dov<u>eh</u>

When will he/she be back?
Quando tornerà?
kw<u>a</u>ndo tornair<u>a</u>

Could you leave him/her a message?
Potrebbe lasciargli/lasciarle un messaggio?
potr<u>e</u>b-be lash<u>a</u>rl-yee/lash<u>a</u>rle oon mes-s<u>a</u>j-jo

I'll call back later
Richiamero più tardi
reekeeah-mayro p-yoo t<u>a</u>rdee

Sorry, I've got the wrong number
Mi scusi, ho sbagliato numero
mee sk<u>oo</u>zee oh zbal-y<u>a</u>to n<u>oo</u>mairo

What's your fax number/email address?
Qual'è il suo numero di fax/posta elettronica?
kwal-<u>ai</u> eel soo-o noo-mairo dee fax/p<u>o</u>sta ai-lait-tronee-ka

Did you get my fax/email?
Ha/hai ricevuto il mio fax/la mia posta elettronica?
a/aee ree-ceh-voo-to eel mee-o fax/p<u>o</u>sta ai-lait-tronee-ka

Please resend your fax
Mi rimanda il suo/mi rimandi il tuo fax, per favore
mee ree-m<u>a</u>nda eel soo-o/mee ree-m<u>a</u>ndee eel too-o fax, pair fav<u>o</u>re

Can I send an email/fax from here?
Posso inviare della posta elettronica/un fax da qui?
p<u>o</u>s-so eenvee-arai del-la p<u>o</u>sta ai-lait-tronee-ka/oon fax d<u>a</u> kwee

Can I use the photocopier/fax machine?
Posso usare la fotocopiatrice/il fax?
p<u>o</u>s-so oosarai la f<u>o</u>tokopee-atreece/eel fax

THE ALPHABET

a	*ah*	h	*ak-ka*	o	*o*	v	*voo*
b	*bee*	i	*ee*	p	*pee*	w	*voo dopp-yo*
c	*chee*	j	*ee-loonga*	q	*koo*	x	*eeks*
d	*dee*	k	*kap-pa*	r	*air-e*	y	*eepseelon*
e	*ay*	l	*el-le*	s	*es-se*	z	*tse-ta*
f	*ef-fe*	m	*em-me*	t	*tee*		
g	*jee*	n	*en-ne*	u	*oo*		

THINGS YOU'LL SEE

apparecchio	phone
centralino	local exchange, operator
chiamata	call
chiamata in teleselezione	direct dialing
chiamata interurbana	long-distance call
chiamata urbana	local call
fuori servizio	out of order
gettoni	telephone tokens
guida telefonica	phone book
il servizio è gratuito	free service
indirizzo di posta elettronica	email address
inserire le monete	insert coins
moneta	coin
numeri utili	useful numbers
Pagine Gialle	Yellow Pages
prefissi telefonici	area codes
riagganciare	hang up
ricevitore	receiver
scatto	unit
selezionare il numero	dial the number
servizio guasti	faulty service
sollevare	to lift
telefonino	mobile phone

THINGS YOU'LL HEAR

Pronto
Hello

Sono io/pronto
Speaking

Con chi vuole parlare?
Whom would you like to speak to?

Ha sbagliato numero
You've got the wrong number

Chi parla?
Who's calling?

Attenda in linea, prego
Hold, please

Mi dispiace, non c'è
I'm sorry, he/she's not in

Posso richiamarla?
Can I call you back?

Che numero ha?
What is your number?

Tornerà alle …
He/she'll be back at … o'clock

Richiami domani, per favore
Please call again tomorrow

Gli dirò che ha chiamato
I'll tell him you called

EMERGENCIES

Information on local health services can be obtained from tourist information offices, but in an emergency dial 113, which is a general emergency number. Dial 115 for the fire department and 118 for an ambulance.

Remember that there is more than one type of police force in Italy: **carabinieri** are a military force and **polizia** are a civil force dealing with crime. In case of emergency, dial either 113 for **polizia** or 112 for **carabinieri**.

For emergency breakdown services, dial 116 (or 01 in the provinces of Potenza, Catanzaro, Lecce, or Caltanisetta). You will be put in touch with the **ACI** (Italian Automobile Club), which will provide immediate assistance. (Also see Driving, page 37.)

USEFUL WORDS AND PHRASES

accident	l'incidente	*eencheedente*
ambulance	l'ambulanza	*amboolantza*
assault	aggredire	*ag-gredeere*
breakdown	il guasto	*gwasto*
break down *(verb)*	guastarsi	*gwastarsee*
burglar	il ladro	*ladro*
burglary	il furto	*foorto*
crash *(noun)*	l'incidente	*eencheedente*
(verb)	avere un incidente	*avaire oon eencheedente*
emergency	l'emergenza	*emairjentza*
emergency room	il pronto soccorso	*pronto so-korso*
fire *(flames)*	il fuoco	*fwoko*
(event)	l'incendio	*eenchend-yo*
fire department	i vigili del fuoco	*veejeelee del fwoko*
flood	l'inondazione	*eenondatz-yone*
injured	ferito	*faireeto*
lose	perdere	*pairdaire*

passport	il passaporto	*pas-saporto*
pickpocket	il borsaiolo	*borsi-olo*
police	la polizia	*poleetzee-a*
police station	il commissariato di polizia	*kom-mees-sar-yato dee poleetzee-a*
rob	derubare	*dairoobare*
steal	rubare	*roobare*
theft	il furto	*foorto*
thief	il ladro	*ladro*
tow	rimorchiare	*reemork-yare*

Help!
Aiuto!
I-ooto

Look out!
(Stia) attento!
(stee-a) at-tento

Stop!
Si fermi!
see fairmee

Where is the US embassy?
Dov'e l'ambasciata americana?
doveh l'amba-shata ameree-kana

This is an emergency!
Questa è un'emergenza!
kwesta eh oon emairjentza

Get an ambulance!
Chiami un'ambulanza!
k-yamee oon amboolantza

Hurry up!
Presto!
presto

Please send an ambulance to …
Per favore, mandate un'ambulanza a …
pair favore mandate oon amboolantza a

Please come to …
Venite, per favore, a …
veneete pair favore a

My address is …
Il mio indirizzo è …
eel mee-o eendeereetzo eh

We've had a break-in
Ci sono entrati i ladri in casa
chee sono entratee ee ladree een kaza

There's a fire at …
C'è un incendio a …
cheh oon eenchend-yo a

Someone's been injured
C'è un ferito
cheh oon faireeto

Someone's been knocked down
È stata investita una persona
eh stata eenvesteeta oona pairsona

He's passed out
È svenuto
eh svenooto

My passport/car has been stolen
Mi hanno rubato il passaporto/la macchina
mee an-no roobato eel pas-saporto/la mak-keena

I've lost my traveler's checks
Ho perso i miei traveller's cheques
o pairso ee mee-ay 'traveler's cheques'

I want to report a stolen credit card
Vorrei denunciare il furto di una carta di credito
vor-ray denoonchare eel foorto dee oona karta dee kredeeto

It was stolen from my room
È stato rubato dalla mia camera
eh stato roobato dal-la mee-a kamaira

I lost it in the park/at the station
L'ho perso nel parco/alla stazione
lo pairso nel parko/al-la statz-yone

My luggage is missing
I miei bagagli sono spariti
ee mee-ay bagal-yee sono spareetee

Has my luggage been found yet?
Sono stati ritrovati i miei bagagli?
sono statee reetrovatee ee mee-ay bagal-yee

I've crashed my car/had a crash
Ho avuto un incidente con la macchina
oh avooto oon eencheedente kon la mak-keena

My car's been broken into
La mia macchina è stata forzata
la mee-a mak-keena eh stata fortzata

The registration number is …
Il numero di targa è …
eel noomairo dee targa eh

I've been mugged (*said by a man*)
Sono stato aggredito
sono stato ag-gredeeto

(*said by a woman*)
Sono stata aggredita
sono stata ag-gredeeta

My son's missing
Mio figlio è scomparso
m<u>ee</u>-o f<u>ee</u>l-yo eh skomp<u>a</u>rso

He has fair/brown hair
Ha i capelli biondi/castani
a ee kap<u>e</u>l-lee b-y<u>o</u>ndee/kast<u>a</u>nee

He's … years old
Ha … anni
a … <u>a</u>n-nee

I've locked myself out *(said by a man)*
Sono rimasto chiuso fuori
s<u>o</u>no reem<u>a</u>sto k-y<u>oo</u>zo fw<u>o</u>ree

(said by a woman)
Sono rimasta chiusa fuori
s<u>o</u>no reem<u>a</u>sta k-y<u>oo</u>za fw<u>o</u>ree

He's drowning!
Sta annegando!
sta an-neg<u>a</u>ndo

He/she can't swim!
Non sa nuotare!
non sa nwot<u>a</u>re

THINGS YOU'LL HEAR

Il suo/vostro indirizzo, prego?
What's your address, please?

Dove si trova/vi trovate?
Where are you?

Può descriverlo?
Can you describe it/him?

THINGS YOU'LL SEE

carabinieri	police
commissariato di polizia	police station
emergenza sanitaria	medical emergency
farmacia di turno	pharmacy on duty
numeri di emergenza	emergency phone numbers
ospedale	hospital
polizia	police
polizia stradale	traffic police
pronto intervento	emergency service
pronto soccorso	first aid, casualty
soccorso alpino	mountain rescue
soccorso stradale	breakdown service
telefono	telephone
vigili del fuoco	fire department

HEALTH

If you are in need of urgent medical attention, go to the **Pronto Soccorso** (emergency room) of the nearest hospital. Visitors from the US should check with their insurance companies before leaving to be sure that they are covered for medical care in Italy. If you need care, remember to get an itemized bill to submit to your insurance company. In some cases, insurance companies will require an official translation before they will reimburse you. Travelers may also wish to take out additional private travel insurance.

Various medicines are available in any pharmacy (**farmacia**), but a prescription may be required. Because of 24-hour service, there is always a pharmacy open in all cities and most towns. Those that are open at night (**servizio notturno**) are listed in local newspapers and on all pharmacy doors.

USEFUL WORDS AND PHRASES

accident	l'incidente	*eencheedente*
adhesive bandage	il cerotto	*chairot-to*
ambulance	l'ambulanza	*amboolantza*
anemic	anemico	*anemeeko*
appendicitis	l'appendicite	*ap-pendeecheete*
appendix	l'appendice	*ap-pendeeche*
aspirin	l'aspirina	*aspeereena*
asthma	l'asma	*azma*
backache	il mal di schiena	*mal dee sk-yena*
bandage	la fascia, benda	*fasha, benda*
bite (*by dog, snake*)	il morso	*morso*
(*by insect*)	la puntura	*poontoora*
bladder	la vescica	*vesheeka*
blister	la vescica	*vesheeka*
blood	il sangue	*sangwe*
blood donor	il donatore di sangue	*donatore dee sangwe*
burn	la bruciatura	*broo-chatoora*

113

cancer	il cancro	_kankro_
chest	il petto	_pet-to_
chicken pox	la varicella	_vareechel-la_
cold	il raffreddore	_raf-fred-dore_
concussion	la commozione cerebrale	_kom-motz-yone chairebrale_
constipation	la stitichezza	_steeteeketza_
contact lenses	le lenti a contatto	_lentee a kontat-to_
corn	il callo	_kal-lo_
cough	la tosse	_tos-se_
cut	il taglio	_tal-yo_
dentist	il dentista	_denteesta_
diabetes	il diabete	_dee-abete_
diarrhea	la diarrea	_dee-are-a_
doctor	il dottore, il medico	_dot-tore, medeeko_
earache	il mal d'orecchi	_mal dorek-kee_
fever	la febbre	_feb-bre_
filling	l'otturazione	_ot-tooratz-yone_
first aid	il pronto soccorso	_pronto sok-korso_
flu	l'influenza	_eenfloo-entza_
fracture	la frattura	_frat-toora_
German measles	la rosolia	_rozolee-a_
hangover	la sbornia	_sborneea_
hay fever	il raffreddore da fieno	_raf-fred-dore da f-yeno_
headache	il mal di testa	_mal dee testa_
heart	il cuore	_kwore_
heart attack	l'infarto	_eenfarto_
hemorrhage	l'emorragia	_emor-rajee-a_
hepatitis	l'epatite	_epatitee_
HIV positive	HIV positivo	_HIV positivo_
hospital	l'ospedale	_ospedale_
indigestion	l'indigestione	_eendeejest-yone_
injection	l'iniezione	_een-yetz-yone_
itch	il prurito	_prooreeto_
kidney	il rene	_rene_

lump	il nodulo	_nodoolo_
measles	il morbillo	_morbeel-lo_
migraine	l'emicrania	_emeekranee-a_
mumps	gli orecchioni	_orekk-yonee_
nausea	la nausea	_now-ze-a_
nurse	l'infermiera	_eenfairmee-aira_
(male)	l'infermiere	_eenfairmee-aire_
operation	l'operazione	_opairatz-yone_
optician	l'ottico	_ot-teeko_
pain	il dolore	_dolore_
penicillin	la penicillina	_peneecheel-leena_
pharmacy	il farmacista	_farmacheesta_
plaster of Paris	il gesso	_jes-so_
pneumonia	la polmonite	_polmoneete_
pregnant	incinta	_eencheenta_
prescription	la ricetta	_reechet-ta_
rheumatism	il reumatismo	_re-oomateezmo_
scald	la scottatura	_skot-tatoora_
scratch	il graffio	_graf-fee-o_
sick	malato	_malato_
smallpox	il vaiolo	_vi-olo_
sore throat	il mal di gola	_mal dee gola_
splinter	la scheggia	_skej-ja_
sprain	la slogatura,	_zlogatura,_
	lo strappo	_strap-po_
	muscolare	_mooskolare_
sting	la puntura	_poontura_
stomach	lo stomaco	_stomako_
temperature	la febbre	_feb-bre_
tonsils	le tonsille	_tonseel-le_
toothache	il mal di denti	_mal dee dentee_
travel sickness	il mal d'auto	_mal dowto_
ulcer	l'ulcera	_oolchaira_
vaccination	la vaccinazione	_vacheenatz-yone_
vomit (verb)	vomitare	_vomeetare_
whooping cough	la pertosse	_pairtos-se_

I have a pain in …
Mi fa male …
mee fa male

I do not feel well
Non mi sento bene
non mee sento bene

I feel faint
Mi sento svenire
mee sento zveneere

I feel sick
Ho la nausea
o la now-ze-a

I feel dizzy
Mi gira la testa
mee jeera la testa

It hurts here
Mi fa male qui
mee fa male kwee

It's a sharp/dull pain
È un dolore acuto/sordo
eh oon dolore akooto/sordo

It hurts all the time
Mi fa continuamente male
mee fa konteenoo-amente male

It only hurts now and then
Non mi fa sempre male
non mee fa sempre male

It hurts when you touch it
Mi fa male quando lo tocca
mee fa male kwando lo tok-ka

It hurts more at night
Mi fa male di più di notte
mee fa male dee p-yoo dee not-te

It stings
Brucia
broocha

It aches
Fa male
fa male

I have a temperature
Ho la febbre
o la feb-bre

I'm ... months pregnant
Sono incinta di ... mesi
sono eencheenta dee ... maisee

Can you take these if you're pregnant/breastfeeding?
Va bene prendere queste quando si è incinta/si sta allattando?
va bene prendaire kwe-ste kwando see e eencheenta/see sta al-lat-tando

I need a prescription for ...
Avrei bisogno di una ricetta per ...
avray beezon-yo dee oona reechet-ta pair

I normally take ...
Generalmente prendo ...
jenairalmente prendo

I'm allergic to ... *(said by a man/woman)*
Sono allergico/allergica a ...
sono al-lairjeeko/al-lairjeeka a

Have you got anything for ...?
Ha qualcosa per ...?
a kwalkoza pair

Do I need a prescription for ...?
C'è bisogno della ricetta per ...?
cheh beezon-yo del-la reechet-ta pair

I have lost a filling
Ho perso un'otturazione
oh pairso oon ot-tooratz-yone

Will he/she be all right?
Starà bene?
stara bene

Will he/she need an operation?
Dovrà essere operato/operata?
dovra essaire operato/operata

How is he/she?
Come sta?
kome sta

THINGS YOU'LL SEE

ambulanza	ambulance
anticamera	waiting room
autoambulanza	ambulance
chirurgia	surgery
chirurgo	surgeon
degente	inpatient
dermatologo	dermatologist
dottore	doctor
farmacia di turno	late-night pharmacy
ginecologo	gynecologist
infermeria	infirmary
medico di turno	doctor on duty
oculista	ophthalmologist
orario di visita	visiting hours
ospedale	hospital

→

otorinolaringoiatra	ear, nose, and throat specialist
ottico	optician
pronto soccorso	first aid, emergency room
reparto	ward
sala operatoria	operating room
specialista	specialist

THINGS YOU'LL HEAR

Da inghiottire con acqua
To be swallowed with water

Da masticare
Chew them

Una/due/tre volte al giorno
Once/twice/three times a day

Prima di andare a letto
At bedtime

Al mattino
In the morning

Cosa prende normalmente?
What do you normally take?

Penso che lei debba andare dal medico
I think you should see a doctor

Mi dispiace, non ne abbiamo/vendiamo
I'm sorry, we don't have/sell that

Per questo c'è bisogno della ricetta
You need a prescription for that

CONVERSION TABLES

DISTANCES

A mile is 1.6 km. To convert kilometers to miles, divide the km by 8 and multiply by 5. Convert miles to km by dividing the miles by 5 and multiplying by 8.

miles	0.62	1.24	1.86	2.43	3.11	3.73	4.35	6.21
miles *or* km	1	2	3	4	5	6	7	10
km	1.61	3.22	4.83	6.44	8.05	9.66	11.27	16.10

WEIGHTS

The kilogram is equivalent to 2 lb 3 oz. To convert kg to lbs, divide by 5 and multiply by 11. One ounce is about 28 grams, and eight ounces about 227 grams; 1 lb is therefore about 454 grams.

lbs	2.20	4.41	6.61	8.82	11.02	13.23	19.84	22.04
lbs *or* kg	1	2	3	4	5	6	9	10
kg	0.45	0.91	1.36	1.81	2.27	2.72	4.08	4.53

TEMPERATURE

To convert Celsius degrees into Fahrenheit, the accurate method is to multiply the C° figure by 1.8 and add 32. Similarly, to convert F° to C°, subtract 32 from the F° figure and divide by 1.8.

C°	-10	0	5	10	20	30	36.9	40	100
F°	14	32	41	50	68	86	98.4	104	212

LIQUIDS

A liter is about 2.1 pints; a gallon is roughly 3.8 liters.

gals	0.27	0.53	1.33	2.65	5.31	7.96	13.26
gals *or* liters	1	2	5	10	20	30	50
liters	3.77	7.54	18.85	37.70	75.40	113.10	188.50

TIRE PRESSURES

lb/sq in	18	20	22	24	26	28	30	33
kg/sq cm	1.3	1.4	1.5	1.7	1.8	2.0	2.1	2.3

MINI-DICTIONARY

a un/uno/una/un' *(see page 5)*
about: about 16 circa 16
  a book about Venice
  un libro su Venezia
absorbent cotton il cotone idrofilo
accelerator l'acceleratore
accident l'incidente
accommodations l'alloggio,
  il posto
ache il dolore
adaptor il riduttore
address l'indirizzo
adhesive l'adesivo
admission charge prezzo d'ingresso
after dopo
afternoon il pomeriggio
aftershave il dopobarba
again di nuovo
against contro
AIDS l'Aids
air l'aria
air conditioning
  l'aria condizionata
aircraft l'aereo
airline la linea aerea
airport l'aeroporto
airport shuttle l'autobus navetta
alarm clock la sveglia
alcohol l'alcol
all tutto
  all the streets
  tutte le strade
  that's all questo è tutto
almost quasi
alone solo
Alps le Alpi
already già
always sempre

am: I am (io) sono
ambulance l'ambulanza
America l'America
American *(man)* l'americano
  (woman) l'americana
  (adj.) americano
and e
ankle la caviglia
another un altro, un'altra
answering machine la segreteria
  telefonica
antifreeze l'antigelo
antiques shop il negozio
  di antiquariato
antiseptic l'antisettico
apartment l'appartamento
aperitif l'aperitivo
appetite l'appetito
apple la mela
application form il modulo
  per la domanda
appointment l'appuntamento
apricot l'albicocca
are: you are (Lei) è
  (singular, familiar) (tu) sei
  (plural) (voi) siete
  we are (noi) siamo
  they are (loro) sono
arm il braccio
arrive arrivare
art l'arte
art gallery la galleria d'arte
artist l'artista
as: as soon as possible
  (il) più presto possibile
ashtray il portacenere
asleep: he's asleep dorme
aspirin l'aspirina

at: at the post office all'ufficio postale
  at night di notte
  at 3 o'clock alle tre
ATM lo sportello automatico
attractive attraente
aunt la zia
Australia l'Australia
Australian *(man)* l'australiano
  (woman) l'australiana
  (adj.) australiano
automatic automatico
away: is it far away? è lontano?
  go away! vattene!
awful terribile, orribile
axle il semiasse

baby il bambino
  (female) la bambina
baby carriage la carrozzina
baby wipes i fazzolettini igienici
back *(not front)* la parte posteriore
  (body) la schiena
  to come back tornare
backpack lo zaino
bacon la pancetta
  bacon and eggs uova e pancetta
bad cattivo
bag la borsa
baggage claim il ritiro bagagli
bait l'esca
bake cuocere (al forno)
bakery la panetteria
balcony il balcone
ball *(soccer, etc.)* la palla, il pallone
  (tennis, etc.) la pallina
ballpoint pen Biro®
banana la banana
band *(musicians)* la banda
bandage la fascia
  (adhesive) il cerotto
bangs *(hair)* la frangia
bank la banca

bar *(drinks)* il bar
  bar of chocolate la tavoletta di cioccolata
barbecue il barbecue
  (occasion) la grigliata all'aperto
barbershop il barbiere
bargain l'affare
basement il seminterrato
basket il cestino
  (in supermarket) il cestello
bath il bagno
  (tub) la vasca da bagno
  to take a bath fare il bagno
bathroom il bagno
battery la batteria
beach la spiaggia
beans i fagioli
beard la barba
beautiful bello
because perché
bed il letto
bed linen le lenzuola
bedroom la camera da letto
beef il manzo
beer la birra
before ... prima di ...
beginner il/la principiante
beginners' slope la discesa per principianti
behind dietro
  behind ... dietro a ...
beige beige
bell *(church)* la campana
  (door) il campanello
below sotto
belt la cintura
  (technical) la cinghia
beside ... vicino a ...
best il migliore
better (than) migliore (di)
between ... fra ...
bicycle la bicicletta
big grande

bikini il bikini
bill *(money)* la banconota
bird l'uccello
birthday il compleanno
   happy birthday! buon compleanno!
bite *(noun: by dog)* il morso
   (by insect) la puntura
   (verb: by dog) mordere
   (by insect) pungere
bitter amaro
black nero
blackberry la mora
black currant il ribes nero
blanket la coperta
bleach la varecchina
   (verb: hair) ossigenare
blind *(cannot see)* cieco
   (on window) la tenda avvolgibile
blizzard la bufera di neve
blond *(adj.)* biondo/bionda
blood il sangue
blouse la camicetta
blue azzurro
   (navy blue) blu
boat la nave
   (small) la barca
   (passenger) il battello
body il corpo
boil *(verb: of water)* bollire
bolt *(noun: on door)* il catenaccio
   (verb) chiudere con il catenaccio
bone l'osso
   (fish) la lisca
book *(noun)* il libro
   (verb) prenotare
bookstore la libreria
boot lo stivale
border il confine
boring noioso
born: I was born in America
   sono nato a America
born: I was born in 1965
   sono nato nel 1965

both: both of them tutti e due
   both ... and ... sia ... che ...
bottle la bottiglia
bottle opener l'apribottiglie
bottom il fondo
   (part of body) il sedere
bowl la scodella, la ciotola
   (mixing bowl) la terrina
box la scatola
   (of wood, etc.) la cassetta
box office il botteghino
boy il ragazzo
boyfriend il ragazzo
bra il reggiseno
bracelet il braccialetto
brake *(noun)* il freno
   (verb) frenare
bread il pane
breakdown *(car)* il guasto
   (nervous) l'esaurimento nervoso
   I've had a breakdown *(car)* ho avuto
   un guasto
breakfast la colazione
breathe respirare
bridge il ponte
   the Bridge of Sighs il Ponte dei Sospiri
briefcase la cartella
British britannico
brochure l'opuscolo
broiler la griglia
broken rotto
   broken leg la gamba rotta
brooch la spilla
brother il fratello
brown marrone
bruise il livido
brush *(noun: hair)* la spazzola
   (paint) il pennello
   (cleaning) la scopa
   (verb: hair) spazzolare
bucket il secchio
building l'edificio
bumper il paraurti

burglar il ladro
burn *(noun)* la bruciatura
  (verb) bruciare
bus l'autobus
  (long distance) la corriera
business l'affare
  it's none of your business
  non sono affari tuoi
bus station la stazione degli autobus
  la stazione delle corriere
busy *(place)* animato
but ma
butcher shop la macelleria
butter il burro
button il bottone
buy comprare
by: by the window vicino alla finestra
  by Friday entro venerdì
  by myself da solo
  written by … scritto da …

cabbage il cavolo
cabinet l'armadio
cable car la funivia
cable/satellite TV TV cavo/satellite
café il caffè, il bar
cake la torta
calculator il calcolatore
call: what's it called? come si chiama?
camcorder la videocamera
camera la macchina fotografica
camper *(trailer)* la roulotte
campground il campeggio
camshaft l'albero a camme
can *(vessel)* la lattina
can: can I have …? posso avere …?
  can you …? potreste …?
  he/she can't … non può …
Canada il Canada
Canadian *(man)* il canadese
  (woman) la canadese
  (adj.) canadese

canal il canale
candle la candela
candy la caramella
canoe la canoa
can opener l'apriscatole
cap *(bottle)* il tappo
  (hat) il berretto
car l'auto, la macchina
carbonated frizzante
carburetor il carburatore
card *(for birthday, etc.)* il biglietto di auguri
  playing cards le carte da gioco
cardigan il cardigan
careful attento
  be careful!
  stia attento!
caretaker il portinaio
  (female) la portinaia
carpet il tappeto
carrot la carota
carry out: to carry out da portare via
car seat *(for a baby)* il seggiolino per
  macchina
case *(suitcase)* la valigia
cash *(noun)* il denaro, gli spicci
  (verb) riscuotere
  to pay cash pagare in contanti
cassette la cassetta
cassette player il mangianastri
castle il castello
cat il gatto
cathedral la cattedrale
Catholic cattolico
cauliflower il cavolfiore
cave la grotta
cemetery il cimitero
center il centro
central heating il riscaldamento centrale
certificate il certificato
chair la sedia
change *(noun: money)* il cambio, gli spicci
change *(verb: money, trains)* cambiare
  (clothes) cambiarsi

check l'assegno
  (in restaurant) il conto
checkbook il libretto degli assegni
check-in il check-in
check in (verb) fare il check-in
cheers! (toast) alla salute!, cin cin!
cheese il formaggio
cherry la ciliegia
chess gli scacchi
chest (part of body) il petto
  (furniture) il baule
chest of drawers il cassettone
chewing gum il chewing-gum
chicken il pollo
child il bambino
  (female) la bambina
children i bambini
china la porcellana
chocolate la cioccolata
  box of chocolates una scatola di
  cioccolatini
chop (food) la costoletta
  (verb: cut) tagliare (a pezzetti)
church la chiesa
cigar il sigaro
cigarette la sigaretta
city la città
city center il centro (della città)
class la classe
classical music la musica classica
clean (adj.) pulito
clear (obvious) chiaro
  (water) limpido
clever bravo, intelligente
clock l'orologio
close (near) vicino (a)
  (stuffy) soffocante
  (verb) chiudere
closed chiuso
clothes i vestiti
clubs (cards) fiori
clutch la frizione
coat il capotto

coat hanger l'attaccapanni
cockroach lo scarafaggio
coffee il caffè
coin la moneta
cold (illness) il raffreddore
  (adj.) freddo
  I have a cold ho un raffreddore
Coliseum il Colosseo
collar il colletto
  (for dog) il collare
colleague il collega
collection (stamps, etc.) la collezione
  (postal) la levata
color il colore
color film il rullino a colori
comb (noun) il pettine
  (verb) pettinare
come venire
  I come from ... sono di ...
  we came last week siamo arrivati la
  settimana scorsa
  come here! vieni qui!
comforter il piumino
compact disc il compact disc
compartment lo scompartimento
complicated complicato
computer il computer
concert il concerto
conditioner (hair) il balsamo
condom il preservativo
conductor (bus) il bigliettaio
  (orchestra) il direttore
congratulations! congratulazioni!
consulate il consolato
contact lenses le lenti a contatto
contraceptive il contraccettivo
cook (noun) il cuoco
  (female) la cuoca
  (verb) cucinare
cookie il biscotto
cooking utensils
  gli utensili da cucina
cool fresco

125

cork il tappo
corkscrew il cavatappi
corner l'angolo
corridor il corridoio
cosmetics i cosmetici
cost *(verb)* costare
   what does it cost? quanto costa?
cotton il cotone
cotton balls il cotone idrofilo
cough *(noun)* la tosse
   (verb) tossire
cough drops le pasticche per la gola
country *(state)* il paese
   (not town) la campagna
cousin il cugino
   (female) la cugina
crab il granchio
cramp il crampo
crayfish il gambero
crazy pazzo
cream *(for cake, etc.)* la crema, la panna
   (lotion) la crema
credit card la carta di credito
crew l'equipaggio
crowded affollato
cruise la crociera
crutches le stampelle
cry *(verb: weep)* piangere
   (shout) gridare
cucumber il cetriolo
cuff links i gemelli
cup la tazza
curlers i bigodini
curls i ricci
curry il curry
curtain la tenda
customs la dogana
cut *(noun)* il taglio
   (verb) tagliare

dad il papà, il babbo
damp umido

dance *(noun)* il ballo
   (verb) ballare
dangerous pericoloso
dark scuro
daughter la figlia
day il giorno
dead morto
deaf sordo
dear caro
debit card la carta assegni
deck of cards il mazzo di carte
deep profondo
delayed in ritardo
deliberately deliberatamente
dentist il/la dentista
dentures la dentiera
deodorant il deodorante
department store
   il grande magazzino
departure la partenza
departure lounge la sala d'attesa
develop *(film)* sviluppare
diamond *(jewel)* il diamante
diapers i pannolini
   (disposable) i pannolini usa e getta
diary il diario
dictionary il dizionario
die morire
diesel il diesel
different diverso
   that's different! è diverso!
   I'd like a different one
   ne vorrei un altro
difficult difficile
dining room la sala da pranzo
dinner la cena
dirty sporco
disabled invalido
dishtowel lo strofinaccio
dishwasher la rondella
dishwashing detergent il detersivo
   liquido per piatti
distributor *(in car)* il distributore

dive *(noun)* il tuffo
  (verb) tuffarsi
diving board il trampolino
divorced divorziato
do fare
  how do you do? piacere di conoscerla
dock il molo
doctor il dottore
  (female) la dottoressa
document il documento
dog il cane
doll la bambola
dollar il dollaro
door la porta
double room la camera doppia
doughnut il krapfen
down giù
dress il vestito
drink *(noun)* la bibita
  (verb) bere
  would you like a drink? vorresti
  qualcosa da bere?
drinking water l'acqua potabile
drive *(verb)* guidare
driver il guidatore
  (female) la guidatrice
  (of bus, truck, etc.) l'autista
driver's license la patente di guida
driving regulations il codice della
  strada
drunk ubriaco
dry asciutto
  (wine) secco
dry cleaner's la lavanderia a secco
during durante
dust cloth lo straccio per la polvere
duty-free il duty free

each *(every)* ogni
  twenty euros each venti euro ciascuno
ear l'orecchio
  ears le orecchie

early presto
earrings gli orecchini
east l'est
easy facile
eat mangiare
egg l'uovo
either: either of them l'uno o l'altro
  either ... or ... o ... o ...
elastic elastico
elbow il gomito
electric elettrico
electricity l'elettricità
elevator l'ascensore
else: something else qualcos'altro
  someone else qualcun'altro
  somewhere else da qualche altra parte
email la posta elettronica
email address l'indirizzo di posta
  elettronica
embarrassing imbarazzante
embassy l'ambasciata
embroidery il ricamo
emergency l'emergenza
emergency brake il freno d'emergenza
emergency exit l'uscita di sicurezza
empty vuoto
end la fine
engaged *(couple)* fidanzato/fidanzata
engine *(car)* il motore
  (train) la locomotiva
England l'Inghilterra
English inglese
Englishman l'inglese
Englishwoman l'inglese
enlargement l'ampliamento
enough abbastanza
entrance l'entrata
envelope la busta
eraser la gomma
escalator la scala mobile
especially particolarmente
evening la sera
every ogni

everyone ognuno, tutti
everything tutto
everywhere dappertutto
example l'esempio
  for example per esempio
excellent ottimo, eccellente
excess baggage il bagaglio in eccesso
exchange (*verb*) scambiare
exchange rate il tasso di cambio
excursion l'escursione
excuse me! (*to get past*) permesso!
  (*to get attention*) mi scusi!
  (*when sneezing, etc.*) scusate!
excuse me? prego?
exit l'uscita
expensive caro, costoso
extension cord la prolunga
eye l'occhio
  eyes gli occhi

face la faccia
faint (*unclear*) indistinto
  (*verb*) svenire
fair (*amusement park*) il luna park
  (*trade*) la fiera
  it's not fair non è giusto
false teeth la dentiera
family la famiglia
fan (*ventilator*) il ventilatore
  (*enthusiast*) l'ammiratore
fan belt la cinghia della ventola
fantastic fantastico
far lontano
  how far is it to ...?
  quanto dista da qui ...?
fare la tariffa
farm la fattoria
farmer l'agricoltore
fashion la moda
fast veloce
fat (*person*) grasso
  (*on meat, etc.*) il grasso

father il padre
faucet il rubinetto
fax (*noun*) il fax
  (*verb: document*) spedire via fax
fax machine il fax
feel (*touch*) tastare
  I feel hot ho caldo
  I feel like ... ho voglia di ...
  I don't feel well
  non mi sento bene
felt-tip pen il pennarello
fence lo steccato
ferry il traghetto
fever la febbre
fiancé il fidanzato
fiancée la fidanzata
field il campo
filling (*in tooth*) l'otturazione
  (*in sandwich, cake, etc.*) il ripieno
film (*for camera*) la pellicola
  (*at movies*) il film
filter il filtro
finger il dito
fire il fuoco
  (*blaze*) l'incendio
fire extinguisher l'estintore
fireworks i fuochi d'artificio
first primo
first aid il pronto soccorso
first name il nome di battesimo
fish il pesce
fishing la pesca
  to go fishing andare a pesca
fish market il pescivendolo
flag la bandiera
flash (*camera*) il flash
flashlight la torcia elettrica
flat (*level*) piatto
flavor il gusto
flea la pulce
flight il volo
flip-flops gli infradito
flippers le pinne

floor (*story*) il piano
  (*ground*) il pavimento
flour la farina
Florence Firenze
flower il fiore
flute il flauto
fly (*insect*) la mosca
  (*verb*) volare
  I'm flying to Florence vado a Firenze
  in aereo
fog la nebbia
folk music la musica folk
food il cibo
food poisoning l'intossicazione alimentare
foot il piede
for per
  for me per me
  what for? perché?
foreigner lo straniero, il forestiero
forest la foresta
forget dimenticare
fork (*for food*) la forchetta
fourth quarto
France la Francia
free (*not occupied*) libero
  (*no charge*) gratis
freezer il congelatore
French francese
french fries le patatine fritte
Frenchman il francese
Frenchwoman la francese
friend l'amico
  (*female*) l'amica
friendly cordiale
front: in front of you davanti a te
frost il gelo
fruit la frutta
fruit juice il succo di frutta
fry friggere
frying pan la padella
full pieno
  I'm full (up) sono sazio
full board la pensione completa

funny divertente
  (*odd*) strano
furniture i mobili

garage il garage
garbage le immondizie, la spazzatura
garbage bag il sacchetto per la
  pattumiera
garbage can la pattumiera
garden il giardino
garlic l'aglio
gas la benzina
gas station la stazione di servizio
gate il cancello
  (*at airport*) l'uscita
gay (*homosexual*) omosessuale, gay
gear (*car*) il cambio
gel (*hair*) il gel
Genoa Genova
German (*man*) il tedesco
  (*woman*) la tedesca
  (*adj.*) tedesco
Germany la Germania
get (*obtain*) ricevere
  (*fetch: person*) chiamare
  (*something*) prendere
  have you got …? ha …?
  to get the train prendere il treno
get back: we get back tomorrow
  torniamo domani
  to get something back riavere indietro
  qualcosa
get in entrare
  (*arrive*) arrivare
get off (*bus, etc.*) scendere (da)
get on (*bus, etc.*) salire (su)
get out uscire (da)
get up alzarsi
gift il regalo
gin il gin
ginger (*spice*) lo zenzero
girl la ragazza
girlfriend la ragazza

give dare
glad contento
glass *(material)* il vetro
  (for drinking) il bicchiere
glasses gli occhiali
glossy prints le fotografie su carta
  lucida
gloves i guanti
glue la colla
go andare
  (depart) partire
gold l'oro
good buono
  good! bene!
goodbye arrivederci
government il governo
granddaughter la nipote
grandfather il nonno
grandmother la nonna
grandparents i nonni
grandson il nipote
grapes l'uva
grass l'erba
gray grigio
Great Britain la Gran Bretagna
Greece la Grecia
Greek *(man)* il greco
  (woman) la greca
  (adj.) greco
green verde
grocery store l'alimentari
ground cloth il telone impermeabile
ground floor il pianterreno
guarantee *(noun)* la garanzia
  (verb) garantire
guard la guardia
guide *(person)* la guida
guidebook la guida
guitar la chitarra
gun *(rifle)* il fucile
  (pistol) la pistola

hair i capelli
haircut il taglio
hair dryer il fohn
hair salon il parrucchiere
hairspray la lacca per i capelli
half metà
  half an hour mezz'ora
  half board mezza pensione
ham il prosciutto
hamburger l'hamburger
hammer il martello
hand la mano
hand brake il freno a mano
handle *(door)* la maniglia
handsome bello, attraente
hangover i postumi della sbornia
happy felice
harbor il porto
hard duro
  (difficult) difficile
hardware store la ferramenta
hat il cappello
have avere
  I don't have … non ho …
  have you got …? ha …?
  I have to go now devo andare adesso
he lui
head la testa
headache il mal di testa
headlights i fari
hear udire, sentire
hearing aid l'apparecchio acustico
heart il cuore
hearts *(cards)* cuori
heater il termosifone
heating il riscaldamento
heavy pesante
heel *(of foot)* il tallone
  (of shoe) il tacco
hello ciao
  (on phone) pronto
help *(noun)* l'aiuto
  (verb) aiutare

hepatitis l'epatite

her: it's for her è per lei
  give it to her daglielo
  her book il suo libro

her: her house la sua casa
  her shoes le sue scarpe
  her dresses i suoi vestiti
  it's hers è suo

high alto

highway l'autostrada

hill la collina

him: it's for him è per lui
  give it to him daglielo

his: his book il suo libro
  his house la sua casa
  his shoes le sue scarpe
  his socks i suoi calzini
  it's his è suo

history la storia

hitchhike fare l'autostop

HIV positive HIV positivo

hobby il passatempo

home: at home a casa

homeopathy omeopatia

honest onesto

honey il miele

honeymoon la luna di miele

hood (car) il cofano

horn (car) il clacson
  (animal) il corno

horrible orribile

hospital l'ospedale

hour l'ora

house la casa

how? come?

hungry: I'm hungry ho fame

hurry: I'm in a hurry ho fretta

husband il marito

I io

ice il ghiaccio

ice cream il gelato

ice skates i pattini da ghiaccio

if se

ignition l'accensione

ill malato

immediately immediatamente

impossible impossibile

in: in English in inglese
  in the hotel nell'albergo
  in Venice a Venezia

indigestion l'indigestione

inexpensive economico, a buon mercato

infection l'infezione

information le informazioni

inhaler (for asthma, etc.) l'inalatore

injection l'iniezione

injury la ferita

ink l'inchiostro

inner tube la camera d'aria

insect l'insetto

insect repellent l'insettifugo

insomnia l'insonnia

instant coffee il caffè solubile

insurance l'assicurazione

interesting interessante

internet l'internet

interpreter l'interprete

invitation l'invito

Ireland l'Irlanda

Irish irlandese

Irishman l'irlandese

Irishwoman l'irlandese

iron (material) il ferro
  (for clothes) il ferro da stiro
  (verb) stirare

is: he/she/it is … (lui/lei/esso) è …

island l'isola

it esso

Italian (man) l'italiano
  (woman) l'italiana
  (adj.) italiano
  the Italians gli italiani

Italy Italia

its suo

jacket la giacca
jam la marmellata
jazz il jazz
jeans i jeans
jellyfish la medusa
jeweler il gioielliere
job il lavoro
jog *(verb)* fare jogging
  to jog andare a fare jogging
jogging il jogging
jogging suit la tuta da ginnastica
joke lo scherzo
just *(only)* solo
  it's just arrived è appena arrivato

kettle il bollitore
key la chiave
kidney il rene
kilo il chilo
kilometer il chilometro
kitchen la cucina
knee il ginocchio
knife il coltello
knit lavorare a maglia
knitwear la maglieria
know sapere
  (person) conoscere
  I don't know non so

label l'etichetta
lace il pizzo
laces *(of shoe)* i lacci
lady la signora
lake il lago
lamb l'agnello
lamp la lampada
lampshade il paralume
land *(noun)* la terra
  (verb) atterrare
language la lingua
large grande

last *(final)* ultimo
  last week la settimana scorsa
  at last! finalmente!
last name il cognome
late: it's getting late
  si sta facendo tardi
  the bus is late
  l'autobus è in ritardo
later più tardi
laugh ridere
laundry *(place)* la lavanderia
  (dirty clothes) la biancheria
laundry detergent il detersivo (per
  bucato)
laxative il lassativo
lazy pigro
leaf la foglia
leaflet il volantino
learn imparare
leather la pelle, il cuoio
left *(not right)* sinistra
  there's nothing left
  non c'è rimasto più nulla
leg la gamba
lemon il limone
lemonade la limonata
length la lunghezza
lens la lente
less meno
lesson la lezione
letter la lettera
letter carrier il postino
lettuce la lattuga
library la biblioteca
license la patente
license plate la targa
life la vita
light *(noun)* la luce
  (adj.: not heavy) leggero
  (not dark) chiaro
light bulb la lampadina
lighter l'accendino
lighter fluid il gas per accendini

light meter l'esposimetro
like: I like you mi piaci
  I like swimming mi piace nuotare
  it's like … assomiglia a …
  like this one come questo
lime *(fruit)* il limoncello
line *(noun)* la fila
  (verb) fare la fila
lip balm il burro di cacao
lipstick il rossetto
liqueur il liquore
list l'elenco
liter il litro
litter i rifiuti
little *(small)* piccolo
  it's a little big è un po' grande
  just a little solo un po'
liver il fegato
lollipop il lecca lecca
long lungo
  how long does it take? quanto ci vuole?
long-distance *(call)* interurbana
lounge chair la sedia a sdraio
lost and found office l'ufficio oggetti
  smarriti
lot: a lot molto
loud forte
  (color) vivo
love *(verb)* amare
lover l'amante
low basso
luck la fortuna
  good luck! buona fortuna!
luggage i bagagli
luggage locker il desposito bagagli
luggage rack la reticella (per i bagagli)
lunch il pranzo

magazine la rivista
mail *(noun)* la posta
  (verb) spedire per posta
mailbox la bucca delle lettere

make fare
makeup il trucco
man l'uomo
manager il direttore
  (female) la direttrice
many: not many non molti
map la carta (geografica)
  a map of Rome una piantina di Roma
marble il marmo
margarine la margarina
market il mercato
marmalade la marmellata d'arance
married sposato
mascara il mascara
mass *(church)* la messa
mast l'albero
match *(light)* il fiammifero
  (sport) l'incontro
material *(cloth)* la stoffa
matter: it doesn't matter non importa
mattress il materasso
maybe forse
me: it's me sono io
  it's for me è per me
  give it to me dammelo
meal il pasto
mean: what does this mean?
  che cosa significa?
meat la carne
mechanic il meccanico
medicine la medicina
Mediterranean il Mediterraneo
meeting l'incontro
melon il melone
menu il menù
message il messaggio
middle: in the middle of the square
  in mezzo alla piazza
  in the middle of the night nel cuore
  della notte
midnight mezzanotte
Milan Milano
milk il latte

mine: it's mine è mio
mineral water l'acqua minerale
minute il minuto
mirror lo specchio
Miss Signorina
mistake l'errore
mobile phone il telefonino
modem il modem
mom mamma
money i soldi
month il mese
monument il monumento
moon la luna
moped il motorino
more: more than ... più di ...
  I want some more ne voglio ancora
morning la mattina
  in the morning di mattina
mosaic il mosaico
mosquito la zanzara
mother la madre
motorboat il motoscafo
motorcycle la motocicletta
mountain la montagna
mountain bike il mountain bike
mouse il topo
mousse *(for hair)* la schiuma
mouth la bocca
move *(verb)* muovere
  (move house) traslocare
  don't move! non muoverti!
movie theater il cinema
Mr. Signor
Mrs. Signora
much: much better molto meglio
  much slower molto più lentamente
  not much non molto
mug il tazzone
museum il museo
mushroom il fungo
music la musica
musical instrument lo strumento
  musicale

musician il musicista
mussels le cozze
must: I must devo
mustache i baffi
mustard la senape
my: my book il mio libro
  my bag la mia borsa
  my keys le mie chiavi
  my dresses i miei vestiti

nail *(metal)* il chiodo
  (finger) l'unghia
nail clippers il tagliaunghie
nail file la limetta per le unghie
nail polish lo smalto per le unghie
name il nome
  what's your name? come ti chiami?
napkin gli assorbenti (igienici)
Naples Napoli
narrow stretto
near: near the door vicino alla porta
necessary necessario
neck il collo
necklace la collana
need: I need ... ho bisogno di ...
  there's no need non c'è bisogno
needle l'ago
negative *(photo)* la negativa
  (adj.) negativo
neither: neither of them
  nè l'uno nè l'altro
  neither ... nor
  ... nè ... nè ...
nephew il nipote
never mai
  I never smoke non fumo mai
new nuovo
news le notizie
  (on radio) il notiziario
newspaper il giornale
newsstand il giornalaio
New Zealand la Nuova Zelanda

New Zealander *(man)* il neozelandese
  (woman) la neozelandese
  (adj.) neozelandese
next prossimo
  next week la settimana prossima
  what next? e poi?
  who's next? a chi tocca?
nice *(attractive)* carino, bello
  (pleasant) simpatico
  (to eat) buono
niece la nipote
night la notte
nightclub il night
nightgown la camicia da notte
night porter il portiere di notte
no *(response)* no
  I have no money non ho soldi
nobody nessuno
noisy rumoroso
noon mezzogiorno
north il nord
Northern Ireland l'Irlanda del Nord
nose il naso
not non
  he's not … non è …
notebook il quaderno
nothing niente
novel il romanzo
now ora, adesso
nowhere da nessuna parte
nudist il/la nudista
number il numero
nut la noce, la nocciola
  (for bolt) il dado

oars i remi
occasionally ogni tanto
occupied occupato
octopus la piovra, il polipo
of di
office l'ufficio
often spesso

oil l'olio
ointment l'unguento
OK OK
old vecchio
  how old are you? quanti anni hai?
olive l'oliva
olive oil l'olio d'oliva
omelette l'omelette
on su
  on the table sul tavolo
  a book on Venice un libro su Venezia
  on Monday di lunedì
one uno
one-way ticket il biglietto di sola andata
onion la cipolla
only solo
open *(adj.)* aperto
  (verb) aprire
operation l'operazione
operator l'operatore
  (female) l'operatrice
opposite: opposite the hotel di fronte
  all'albergo
optician l'ottico
or o
orange *(fruit)* l'arancia
  (color) arancione
orange juice il succo d'arancia
orchestra l'orchestra
ordinary normale
organ *(music)* l'organo
other: the other (one) l'altro
our: our hotel il nostro albergo
  our car la nostra macchina
  it's ours è nostro
out: he's out è uscito
outside fuori
oven il forno
over *(above)* su, sopra
  over 100 più di cento
  over the river al di là del fiume
  it's over *(finished)* è finito
  over there laggiù

pacifier *(for baby)* il ciuccio
package il pacchetto
packet il pacchetto
padlock il lucchetto
Padua Padova
page la pagina
pain il dolore
paint la vernice
pair il paio
pajamas il pigiama
palace il palazzo
pale pallido
pants i pantaloni
pantyhose i collant
paper la carta
  (newspaper) il giornale
paraffin la paraffina
parents i genitori
park *(noun)* il parco
  (verb) parcheggiare
parking lights le luci di posizione
parsley il prezzemolo
part *(hair)* la riga
party *(celebration)* la festa
  (group) il gruppo
  (political) il partito
pass *(driving)* sorpassare
passenger il passeggero
  (female) la passeggera
passport il passaporto
pasta la pasta
pastry store la pasticceria
path il sentiero
pay pagare
peach la pesca
peanuts le arachidi
pear la pera
pearl la perla
peas i piselli
pedestrian il pedone
pen la penna
pencil la matita
pencil sharpener il temperamatite

pen pal il/la corrispondente
people la gente
pepper il pepe
  (red, green) il peperone
peppermint la menta piperita
per: per person a persona
  per annum all'anno
perfect perfetto
perfume il profumo
perhaps forse
perm la permanente
pharmacy la farmacia
phone book la guida telefonica
phonecard la scheda telefonica
photocopier la fotocopiatrice
photograph *(noun)* la fotografia
  (verb) fotografare
photographer il fotografo
phrase book il vocabolarietto
pickpocket il borsaiolo
picnic il picnic
piece il pezzo
pill la compressa
pillow il cuscino
pin lo spillo
  (clothes) la molletta
pineapple l'ananas
pink rosa
pipe *(for smoking)* la pipa
  (for water) il tubo
piston il pistone
pizza la pizza
place il posto
  at your place a casa tua
plant la pianta
plastic la plastica
plastic bag il sacchetto di plastica
plastic wrap la pellicola adesiva
plate il piatto
platform il binario
play *(theater)* la commedia
  (verb) giocare
please per favore

plug (*electrical*) la spina
  (*sink*) il tappo
pocket la tasca
pocketbook la borsetta
pocketknife il temperino
poison il veleno
police la polizia
police officer il poliziotto
police station la stazione di polizia
politics la politica
poor povero
  poor quality di cattiva qualità
Pope il Papa
pop music la musica pop
pork la carne di maiale
port il porto
porter (*hotel*) il portiere
possible possibile
postcard la cartolina
poster il manifesto
post office l'ufficio postale
potato la patata
potato chips le patatine
poultry il pollame
pound (*weight*) la libbra
prefer preferire
prescription la ricetta
pretty (*beautiful*) grazioso, carino
  (*quite*) piuttosto
priest il prete
private privato
problem il problema
public pubblico
pull tirare
puncture la foratura
purple viola
purse il borsellino
push spingere
put mettere

quality la qualità
quarter il quarto
question la domanda

quick veloce
quiet tranquillo
quite (*fairly*) abbastanza
  (*fully*) molto

radiator il radiatore
radio la radio
radish il ravanello
railroad la ferrovia
rain la pioggia
rain boots gli stivali do gomma
raincoat l'impermeabile
raisins l'uvetta
rare (*uncommon*) raro
  (*steak*) al sangue
raspberry il lampone
rat il ratto
razor blades le lamette
read leggere
reading lamp la lampada da studio
ready pronto
real estate agent l'agente immobiliare
receipt (*restaurants, hotels*) la ricevuta
  (*shops, bars*) lo scontrino
receptionist il/la receptionist
record (*music*) il disco
  (*sports, etc.*) il record
record store il negozio di dischi
red rosso
refreshments i rinfreschi
refrigerator il frigorifero
relax rilassarsi
religion la religione
remember ricordare
  I don't remember non ricordo
rent (*verb: apartment*) affittare
restroom (*men's*) la toilette degli uomini
  (*women's*) la toilette delle donne
reservation la prenotazione
reservations office la biglietteria
rest (*noun: remainder*) il resto
  (*verb: relax*) riposarsi

137

restaurant il ristorante
return ritornare
  (*give back*) restituire
rice il riso
rich ricco
right (*correct*) giusto, esatto
  (*not left*) destro
ring (*jewelry*) l'anello
ripe maturo
river il fiume
road la strada
rock (*stone*) la roccia
  (*music*) il rock
roll (*bread*) il panino
Roman Forum il Foro Romano
Rome Roma
roof il tetto
room la stanza
  (*space*) lo spazio
rope la corda
rose la rosa
round (*circular*) rotondo
  it's my round tocca a me offrire
round-trip ticket il biglietto di andata
  e ritorno
row remare
rowboat la barca a remi
rubber band l'elastico
ruby (*stone*) il rubino
rug (*mat*) il tappeto
ruins le rovine, i resti
ruler (*for drawing*) la riga
rum il rum
run (*verb*) correre

sad triste
safe (*not dangerous*) sicuro
safety pin la spilla di sicurezza
St. Mark's Square Piazza San Marco
St. Peter's San Pietro
salad l'insalata
salami il salame

sale (*at reduced prices*) i saldi
salmon il salmone
salt il sale
same: the same dress
  lo stesso vestito
  same again, please u
  n altro, per favore
sand la sabbia
sandals i sandali
sand dunes le dune
sandwich il panino
sanitary napkins gli assorbenti (igienici)
Sardinia la Sardegna
sauce la salsa
saucepan la pentola
sauna la sauna
sausage la salsiccia
say dire
  what did you say? che cosa ha detto?
  how do you say …? come si dice …?
scarf la sciarpa
  (*head*) il foulard
school la scuola
scissors le forbici
Scotland la Scozia
Scotsman lo scozzese
Scotswoman la scozzese
Scottish scozzese
screw la vite
screwdriver il cacciavite
sea il mare
seafood i frutti di mare
seat il posto
seat belt la cintura di sicurezza
second secondo
second floor il primo piano
see vedere
  I can't see non vedo
  I see capisco, vedo
sell vendere
separate (*adj.*) separato
separated (*couple*) separati
serious serio

several diversi
sew cucire
shampoo lo shampoo
shave: to shave radersi
shaving cream la schiuma da barba
shawl lo scialle
she lei
sheet il lenzuolo
shell la conchiglia
shellfish *(crabs, etc.)* i crostacei
    (mollusks) i molluschi
sherry lo sherry
ship la nave
shirt la camicia
shoelaces i lacci per le scarpe
shoe polish il lucido per le scarpe
shoes le scarpe
shop il negozio
shopping la spesa
    to go shopping andare a fare acquisti
    (for food) andare a fare la spesa
short corto
shorts gli short,i pantaloncini corti
shoulder la spalla
shower la doccia
    (rain) l'acquazzone
shower gel la docciaschiuma
shutter *(camera)* l'otturatore
    (window) l'imposta, le persiane
Sicily la Sicilia
side *(edge)* il lato
sidewalk il marciapiede
sights: the sights of … le attrazioni
    turistiche di …
silk la seta
silver *(color)* d'argento
    (metal) l'argento
simple semplice
sing cantare
single *(one)* solo
    (unmarried: man) celibe
    (woman) nubile
single room la camera singola

sink il lavabo, il lavandino
sister la sorella
skid slittare
skiing: to go skiing andare a sciare
skin cleanser il latte detergente
ski resort la località sciistica
skirt la gonna
skis gli sci
sky il cielo
sleep *(noun)* il sonno
    (verb) dormire
sleeper car *(on train)* il vagone letto
sleeping bag il sacco a pelo
sleeping pill il sonnifero
slip *(garment)* la sottoveste
slippers le pantofole
slow lento
small piccolo
smell *(noun)* l'odore
    (verb: stink) puzzare
smile *(noun)* il sorriso
    (verb) sorridere
smoke *(noun)* il fumo
    (verb) fumare
snack lo spuntino
sneakers le scarpe da ginnastica
snorkel il boccaglio
snow la neve
so: so good così bene
    not so much non così tanto
soaking solution *(for contact lenses)*
    il liquido per lenti
soap il sapone
soccer *(game)* il calcio
    (ball) il pallone
socks i calzini
soda water l'acqua di seltz
somebody qualcuno
somehow in qualche modo
something qualcosa
sometimes qualche volta
somewhere da qualche parte
son il figlio

song la canzone
sorry! scusi!
  I'm sorry mi dispiace
  sorry? (*pardon*) come?, scusi?
soup la zuppa
south il sud
souvenir il souvenir
spade (*shovel*) la vanga
spades (*cards*) picche
Spain la Spagna
Spanish spagnolo
spare parts (*car*) i pezzi di ricambio
spark plug la candela
speak parlare
  do you speak …? parla …?
  I don't speak … non parlo …
speed la velocità
SPF (sun protection factor) il fattore
  di protezione
spider il ragno
spinach gli spinaci
spoon il cucchiaio
spring (*mechanical*) la molla
  (*season*) la primavera
square (*noun: in town*) la piazza
  (*adj.: shape*) quadrato
staircase la scala
stairs le scale
stamp il francobollo
stapler la cucitrice
star la stella
  (*movie*) la star
start (*noun*) l'inizio
  (*verb*) cominciare
station la stazione
statue la statua
steal rubare
  it's been stolen è stato rubato
steamer (*boat*) la nave a vapore
  (*for cooking*) la pentola a pressione
stick shift la leva del cambio
stockings le calze
stomach lo stomaco

stomachache il mal di stomaco
stop (*noun: bus*) la fermata dell'autobus
  (*verb*) fermare
  stop! alt!, fermo!
storm la tempesta
stove il fornello
strawberry la fragola
stream il ruscello
street la strada
string (*cord*) lo spago
  (*guitar, etc.*) la corda
stroller il passeggino
strong forte
student lo studente
  (*female*) la studentessa
stupid stupido
suburbs la periferia
subway la metropolitana
sugar lo zucchero
suit (*noun*) il completo
  it suits you ti sta bene
suitcase la valigia
sun il sole
sunbathe prendere il sole
sunburn la scottatura
sunglasses gli occhiali da sole
sunny: it's sunny c'è il sole
sunshade l'ombrellone
suntan: to get a suntan abbronzarsi
suntan lotion la lozione solare
suntanned abbronzato
supermarket il supermercato
supper la cena
supplement il supplemento
sure sicuro
  are you sure? sei sicuro?
sweat (*noun*) il sudore
  (*verb*) sudare
sweater il maglione
sweatshirt la felpa
sweet (*not sour*) dolce
swim (*verb*) nuotare
swimming pool la piscina

swimming trunks il costume da bagno
(per uomo)
swimsuit il costume da bagno
Swiss *(man)* lo svizzero
(woman) la svizzera
(adj.) svizzero
switch l'interruttore
Switzerland la Svizzera
synagogue la sinagoga

table il tavolo
taillights i fari posteriori
take prendere
takeoff il decollo
talcum powder il talco
talk *(noun)* la conversazione
(verb) parlare
tall alto
tampons i tamponi
tangerine il mandarino
tapestry l'arazzo
teacher l'insegnante
telephone *(noun)* il telefono
(verb) telefonare
telephone booth la cabina telefonica
telephone call la telefonata
television la televisione
temperature la temperatura
(fever) la febbre
tent la tenda
tent pole il palo della tenda
than di
thank *(verb)* ringraziare
thank you/thanks grazie
that: that one quello
that country quel paese
that man quell'uomo
that woman quella donna
what's that? cos'è quello?
I think that … penso che …
the *(see page 5)*
their: their room la loro stanza

their: their friend il loro amico
their books i loro libri
their pens le loro penne
it's theirs è loro
them: it's for them è per loro
give it to them dallo a loro
then poi, allora
there là
there is/are … c'è/ci sono …
is/are there …? c'è/ci sono …?
these: these things queste cose
these boys questi ragazzi
they loro
thick spesso
thin sottile
think pensare
I think so penso di sì
I'll think about it ci penserò
third terzo
thirsty: I'm thirsty ho sete
this: this one questo
this picture questo quadro
this man quest'uomo
this woman questa donna
what's this? cos'è questo?
this is Mr. … (questo è) il signor …
those: those things quelle cose
those boys quei ragazzi
throat la gola
through attraverso
thumbtack la puntina da disegno
thunderstorm il temporale
Tiber il Tevere
ticket il biglietto
ticket office la biglietteria
tide la marea
tie *(noun)* la cravatta
(verb) legare
tight *(clothes)* stretto
tights *(wool)* la calzamaglia
time il tempo
what's the time? che ore sono?
timetable l'orario

tin la scatola
tip *(money)* la mancia
   (end) la punta
tire *(on wheel)* la gomma
tired stanco
tissues i fazzoletti di carta
to: to America in America
   to the station alla stazione
   to the doctor dal dottore
   to the center in centro
toast il pane tostato
tobacco il tabacco
today oggi
together insieme
toilet la toilette
toilet paper la carta igienica
tomato il pomodoro
tomato juice il succo di pomodoro
tomorrow domani
tongue la lingua
tonic l'acqua tonica
tonight stasera
too *(also)* anche
   (excessively) troppo
tooth il dente
toothache il mal di denti
toothbrush lo spazzolino da denti
toothpaste il dentifricio
tour il giro
tourist il/la turista
tourist office l'ufficio turistico
towel l'asciugamano
tower la torre
   Leaning Tower of Pisa la Torre di Pisa
town la città
town hall il municipio
toy il giocattolo
toy store il negozio di giocattoli
tractor il trattore
tradition la tradizione
traffic il traffico
traffic jam l'ingorgo
traffic lights il semaforo

trailer il rimorchio
train il treno
translate tradurre
translator il traduttore
   (female) la traduttrice
travel agency l'agenzia di viaggio
traveler's check il traveller's cheque
tray il vassoio
tree l'albero
trip il viaggio
truck il camion
true vero
try provare
Turin Torino
turn signal l'indicatore di direzione
tunnel il tunnel
Tuscany la Toscana
tweezers le pinzette
typewriter la macchina da scrivere

umbrella l'ombrello
uncle lo zio
under ... sotto ...
underpants le mutande
undershirt la canottiera
understand capire
   I don't understand non capisco
underwear la biancheria intima
university l'università
unleaded senza piombo
until fino a
unusual insolito
up su
   (upward) verso l'alto
   up there lassù
urgent urgente
us: it's for us è per noi
   give it to us daccelo
use *(noun)* l'uso
   (verb) usare
   it's no use non serve a niente
useful utile

usual solito
usually di solito

vacancy *(room)* la stanza libera
vacation la vacanza
valley la valle
valve la valvola
vanilla la vaniglia
vase il vaso
Vatican City la Città del Vaticano
VCR il videoregistratore
veal la carne di vitello
vegetables la verdura
vegetarian vegetariano
vehicle il veicolo
Venice Venezia
very molto
  very much moltissimo
video *(tape/film)* il video cassetta
view la vista
viewfinder il mirino
villa la villa
village il villaggio
violin il violino
visit *(noun)* la visita
  (verb) andare a trovare
visitor l'ospite
vitamin pill la compressa di vitamine
vodka la vodka
voice la voce

wait aspettare
  wait! aspetta!
waiter il cameriere
  waiter! cameriere!
waiting room la sala d'attesa
waitress la cameriera
  waitress! cameriera!
Wales il Galles
walk *(noun: stroll)* la passeggiata
  (verb) camminare

walk: to go for a walk
  andare a fare una passeggiata
wall il muro
wallet il portafoglio
war la guerra
wardrobe il guardaroba,
  l'armadio
warm caldo
was: I was (io) ero
  he/she/it was (lui/lei/esso) era
wasp la vespa
watch *(noun)* l'orologio
  (verb) guardare
water l'acqua
waterfall la cascata
water heater lo scaldabagno
wave *(noun)* l'onda
  (verb: with hand) salutare
wavy: wavy hair
  i capelli ondulati
we noi
weather il tempo
website il sito internet
wedding il matrimonio
week la settimana
welcome benvenuto
  you're welcome
  di niente, prego
Welsh gallese
Welshman il gallese
Welshwoman la gallese
were: you were (Lei) era
  (singular, familiar) (tu) eri
  (plural) (voi) eravate
  we were (noi) eravamo
  they were (loro) erano
west l'ovest
wet bagnato
what? cosa?
wheel la ruota
wheelchair la sedia a rotelle
when? quando?
where? dove?

143

whether se
which? quale?
whiskey il whisky
white bianco
who? chi?
why? perchè?
wide ampio
wife la moglie
wind il vento
window la finestra
windshield il parabrezza
wine il vino
wing l'ala
with con
without senza
woman la donna
wood (material) il legno
wool la lana
word la parola
work (noun) il lavoro
   (verb) lavorare
   (machine) funzionare
worse peggiore
worst il peggiore
wrench la chiave fissa
wrapping paper la carta da imballaggio
   (for presents) la carta da regalo
wrist il polso
writing paper la carta da scrivere
wrong sbagliato

year l'anno
yellow giallo
yes sì
yesterday ieri
yet ancora
   not yet non ancora
yogurt lo yogurt
you Lei
   (singular, familiar) tu
   (plural) voi
your: (singular, formal)

your book il suo libro
   your shirt la sua camicia
   your pants le sue scarpe
   (singular, familiar)
   your book il tuo libro
   your shirt la tua camicia
   your shoes le tue scarpe
yours: is this yours? è suo?
   (singular, familiar) è tuo?
youth hostel l'ostello della gioventù

zipper la chiusura lampo
zoo lo zoo